D0204922

The National Economy

The National Economy

BRADLEY A. HANSEN

GREENWOOD GUIDES TO BUSINESS AND ECONOMICS
Wesley B. Truitt, Series Editor

GREENWOOD PRESS
WESTPORT, CONNECTICUT • LONDON

Library of Congress Cataloging-in-Publication Data

Hansen, Bradley A., 1963–
  The national economy / Bradley A. Hansen.
    p. cm. — (Greenwood guides to business and economics)
  Includes bibliographical references and index.
  ISBN 0–313–33541–9 (alk. paper)
  1. United States—Economic conditions—2001 2. Capitalism—United States.
I. Title. II. Series.
  HC106.83.H36   2006
  330.973—dc22   2006001120

British Library Cataloguing-in-Publication Data is available.

Library of Congress Catalog Card Number: 2006001120
ISBN: 0–313–33541–9

First published in 2006

Greenwood Press, 88 Post Road West, Westport, CT 06881
An imprint of Greenwood Publishing Group, Inc.
www.greenwood.com

Printed in the United States of America

The paper used in this book complies with the
Permanent Paper Standard issued by the National
Information Standards Organization (Z39.48–1984).

10 9 8 7 6 5 4 3 2 1

Contents

Illustrations

FIGURES

Series Foreword

Scanning the pages of the newspaper on any given day, you'll find headlines like these:

"OPEC Points to Supply Chains as Cause of Price Hikes"
"Business Groups Warn of Danger of Takeover Proposals"
"U.S. Durable Goods Orders Jump 3.3%"
"Dollar Hits Two-Year High Versus Yen"
"Credibility of WTO at Stake in Trade Talks"
"U.S. GDP Growth Slows While Fed Fears Inflation Growth"

If this seems like gibberish to you, then you are in good company. To most people, the language of economics is mysterious, intimidating, impenetrable. But with economic forces profoundly influencing our daily lives, being familiar with the ideas and principles of business and economics is vital to our welfare. From fluctuating interest rates to rising gasoline prices to corporate misconduct to the vicissitudes of the stock market to the rippling effects of protests and strikes overseas or natural disasters closer to home, "the economy" is not an abstraction. As Robert Duvall, president and CEO of the National Council on Economic Education, has forcefully argued, "Young people in our country need to know that economic education is not an option. Economic literacy is a vital skill, just as vital as reading literacy."[1] Understanding economics is a skill that will help you interpret current events that are playing out on a global scale, or in your checkbook, ultimately helping you make wiser choices about how you manage your financial resources—today and tomorrow.

It is the goal of this series, Greenwood Guides to Business and Economics, to promote economic literacy and improve economic decision-making. All seven books in the series are written for the general reader, high school and college student, or the business manager, entrepreneur, or graduate student in business and economics looking for a handy refresher. They have been written by experts in their respective fields for nonexpert readers. The approach throughout is at a "basic" level to maximize understanding and demystify how our business-driven economy really works.

Each book in the series is an essential guide to the topic of that volume, providing an introduction to its respective subject area. The series as a whole constitutes a library of information, up-to-date data, definitions of terms, and resources, covering all aspects of economic activity. Volumes feature such elements as timelines, glossaries, and examples and illustrations that bring the concepts to life and present them in a historical and cultural context.

The selection of the seven titles and their authors has been the work of an Editorial Advisory Board, whose members are the following: Alan Carsrud, Florida International University; Alan Reynolds, Cato Institute; Robert Spich, University of California, Los Angeles; Wesley Truitt, Loyola Marymount University; Walter E. Williams, George Mason University; and Charles Wolf Jr., RAND Corporation.

As series editor, I served as chairman of the Editorial Advisory Board and want to express my appreciation to each of these distinguished individuals for their dedicated service in helping to bring this important series to reality.

The seven volumes in the series are as follows:

The Corporation by Wesley B. Truitt, Loyola Marymount University

Entrepreneurship by Alan L. Carsrud, Florida International University

Globalization by Robert Spich and Christopher Thornberg, UCLA

Income and Wealth by Alan Reynolds, Cato Institute

Money by Mark Dobeck and Euel Elliott, University of Texas at Dallas

The National Economy by Bradley A. Hansen, University of Mary Washington

The Stock Market by Rik W. Hafer, Southern Illinois University–Edwardsville, and Scott E. Hein, Texas Tech University

Special thanks to our senior editor at Greenwood, Nick Philipson, for conceiving the idea of the series and for sponsoring it within Greenwood Press.

The overriding purpose of each of these books and the series as a whole is, as Walter Williams so aptly put it, to "push back the frontiers of ignorance."

Wesley B. Truitt, Series Editor

NOTE

1. Quoted in Gary H. Stern, "Do We Know Enough about Economics?" *The Region*, Federal Reserve Bank of Minneapolis (December 1998).

Preface

In 2003, the United States produced more than $37,748 worth of goods and services for every person in the country. That tallies up to goods and services worth $10.9 trillion. With just 5 percent of the population of the world, the United States produces over 25 percent of the world's output. It produces more each year than all of the less developed countries combined. It produces more than one-third of the output of all the developed countries.

The economy of the United States today is even more remarkable when it is compared with economies of the past. For most of history, economic growth was so slow it was hardly noticeable. Output per person hardly increased at all between A.D. 1 and A.D. 1000. Output per person increased by about 50 percent from A.D. 1000 to 1800. In the late 1700s, the average person in Western Europe or North America still lived fewer than forty years, and in most of those years the average person had little more food, shelter, and clothing than were necessary to survive. In the early 1800s, per capita income in even the wealthiest countries in Western Europe was only about four times that of the poorest countries in the world.

Since 1800, per capita income in the United States has doubled about every forty-two years. In 1848, Karl Marx, the most famous critic of capitalism, declared in his *Communist Manifesto* that capitalism "in its rule of scarce one hundred years, has created more massive and more colossal productive forces than all preceding generations together." Marx pointed out that no one before had even dreamed of such things as steamships, railroads, or the use of chemistry in industry and agriculture. Marx was right, but he did not dream of the changes that were to come in the next 150 years: advances in medicine and science, electricity, telephones, television, computers, travel by aircraft and automobile. By 1900 the average person in the United States could expect to live 47 years, and by 1997 that had increased to 76 years. Per capita income in the United States in 1997 was more than twenty times that of people in the poorest countries in the world.

In just two hundred years the United States, along with most of Europe and Japan, escaped from the widespread poverty that had characterized all of previous history. The most important questions in economics arise from this revolution in economic growth. Why were the United States and other developed countries able to break free from the poverty that had plagued mankind throughout history? Can these countries continue their rapid growth? And why are some countries still unable to break free of poverty?

Questions about long-term growth are the most important questions in economics, but they are not the only economic questions that trouble us. Another set of questions arises from the fact that economic growth has not always been a steady upward climb. Sometimes production decreases and unemployment rises. Sometimes the prices of goods and services increase rapidly. And sometimes production falls and prices rise. These fluctuations in economic activity are called business cycles. Why has the growth of the economy fluctuated like this? Is there anything that can be done to eliminate downturns in the economy? What can be done to prevent prices from increasing rapidly?

Long-term growth and short-run fluctuations are the defining features of the American economy. This book provides an introduction to the American economy for noneconomists, with an emphasis on understanding these two defining features. The technical jargon of economics is avoided whenever possible; it is introduced only to the extent that it is necessary to understand what economists and policy-makers are saying about the economy.

Chapter 1 presents an overview of how market economies such as in the United States work. Chapter 2 examines how we measure economic performance. Chapter 3 provides an explanation of long-term growth. Chapter 4 covers short-run fluctuations. Chapters 5 through 8 each examine the role of one important part of the national economy: business, households, government, and the foreign sector. Sources of information about the American economy and a chronology of important economic events are included, and there is a glossary at the end of the book.

I would like to thank Wesley Truitt and Nick Philipson for inviting me to participate in the Greenwood Guides to Business and Economics series. I also wish to thank the University of Mary Washington for awarding me a one-semester sabbatical to work on this book, and my students and colleagues at Mary Washington, from whom I gained many useful ideas. Thanks to my children Joanna, Ben, Wendy, Heather, and Jonathan for frequently reminding me what's really important and not letting me get too wrapped up in writing a book.

Most of all, thank you to my wife, Mary Eschelbach Hansen, for discussions, suggestions, editing, proofreading, constant encouragement, and her love.

Chronology of American Economic History

1492	Columbus travels to the New World.
1587	Roanoke colony is established and disappears within one year.
1607	Jamestown is established. Fewer than 40 of the 122 settlers are still alive after the second winter.
1619	Twenty slaves arrive in Virginia.
1620	Plymouth colony is founded.
1763	Proclamation line is established, prohibiting settlement west of the Appalachians.
1765	Stamp Act.
1766	Stamp Act is repealed.
1773	Tea Act and "Boston Tea Party."
1774	Quebec Act extends settlement line to the Ohio River.
1776	Declaration of Independence.
	Adam Smith publishes *An Inquiry into the Nature and Causes of the Wealth of Nations.*
1784–89	The Northwest Ordinances settles land disputes between different states and prescribes the method by which the Old Northwest Territory will be settled.
1789	The Federal Constitution is ratified.

1790 Samuel Slater constructs the first mechanized cotton spinning factory in the United States. Slater emigrated from England, bringing the plans in his head.

1791 Alexander Hamilton's *Report on Manufacturers* lays out a plan for government encouragement of industry.

1792 Buttonwood Tree Agreement. New York stock traders adopt rules for trading.

1794 Eli Whitney invents the cotton gin.

1807 Robert Fulton invents the steamboat.

1814 David Ricardo publishes *Principles of Political Economy and Taxation*, explaining the comparative advantage and the benefits of free trade.

The Boston Associates establish a cotton textile mill in Waltham, Massachusetts.

1817–25 The State of New York constructs the Erie Canal.

1819 The Panic of 1819.

1823 Boston Associates establish integrated cotton textile factory, the Lowell Mills.

1824 Eli Whitney begins the manufacture of rifles with interchangeable parts at Harper's Ferry, West Virginia.

1831 The Baltimore and Ohio Railroad begins operation as the first commercial railroad in the United States.

1844 Samuel Morse uses telegraph to communicate between Baltimore and Washington, D.C.

1851 Crystal Palace Exhibition in London, England.

Petroleum refining.

1861–65 Civil War.

1862 Homestead Act grants free land in the West to settlers.

1869 The transcontinental railroad is completed.

1870 Standard Oil Company is established.

1875	Andrew Carnegie opens Edgar Thomson Works.
1878	Edison Electric Light Company founded.
1882	Chinese Exclusion Act.
1887	Interstate Commerce Act creates the Interstate Commerce Commission.
1890	Sherman Antitrust Act is passed.
1895	*United States v. E. C. Knight.* The Supreme Court rules that Sherman Act applies only to interstate commerce, not manufacture within a state.
1900	United States adopts the gold standard.
1904	Pure Food and Drug Act establishes the Food and Drug Administration.
1911	*Standard Oil of New Jersey v. United States.* Standard Oil is broken up. Supreme Court establishes the "rule of reason" that a monopoly has to be achieved by unlawful means in order to violate the Sherman Act.
1913	Henry Ford introduces the assembly line to automobile production. The price of a Model T falls from $800 to $200.
	Sixteenth Amendment is ratified, allowing a federal income tax.
	The Federal Reserve is established.
1914	Clayton Act and Federal Trade Commission Act.
1929	Stock market crash.
1929–39	The Great Depression.
1936	John Maynard Keynes publishes the *General Theory of Employment, Interest, and Money.*
1932	Glass-Steagall Act allows the Federal Reserve to issue notes backed by government securities, not gold.
1933	Federal Deposit Insurance Corporation. Separation of commercial and investment banking.
1934	Securities and Exchange Act.

1935	Social Security Act.
1941–45	World War II.
1946	Employment Act of 1946.
1954	*Brown v. Board of Education* overturns "separate but equal."
1955	Ray Kroc establishes his first McDonald's franchise.
1959	Jack Kilby manufactures an integrated circuit.
1960s	Environmental Protection Agency, Occupational Safety and Health Administration.
1962	Sam Walton establishes the first Wal-Mart.
1965	Medicare is established.
1966	National Highway Traffic Safety Act.
1969	ARPAnet begins operating, eventually becomes the foundation for the Internet.
1970	Occupational Health and Safety Act. Environmental Protection Agency.
1972	Consumer Product Safety Commission.
1973	Yom Kippur War. First oil price shock.
1975	Bill Gates and Paul Allen establish Microsoft.
1979	Iranian revolution. Second oil price shock.
1981–88	Reagan supply-side tax cuts. Federal Reserve chairman Volcker reduces the rate of growth of the money supply and inflation falls from over 10 percent to under 4 percent.
1987	Alan Greenspan succeeds Paul Volcker as chair of the Fed.
1991–2001	Longest economic expansion.
1999	Gramm-Leach-Bliley Act repeals the Glass-Steagall Act, which separated investment and commercial banking.
2001	Terrorists attack the Pentagon and the Twin Towers in New York City.
2002	Sarbanes-Oxley Act.

One

The Market Economy of the United States

In 2002, the United States produced more than $10 trillion worth of goods and services. The Congo produced barely $2 billion worth of goods and services, less than many American corporations. Big or small, all nations face the same basic economic problem—scarcity. If everyone always had as much of everything as they wanted, there would be no economic problems.

Economics is the study of how people choose to use their scarce resources to satisfy their wants. Resources are all the things we use to produce the goods and services that we want. Goods are things we consume that are physical objects we can touch. Services are things we consume that are not physical objects. A car is a good. Car insurance is a service. Questions about the economy ultimately come down to questions about how we choose to use the resources we have to produce the goods and services we want to consume.

SCARCITY AND CHOICE

Resources are divided into three categories: labor, natural resources, and capital. Labor is the human effort required to make things. Natural resources are the things we use from the natural environment: water, land, lumber, minerals, and the like. Capital is the economic term for goods that we make in order to help us make more goods and services in the future. Factories and equipment, computers and software, roads and bridges are all things we make to help us produce even more in the future. They are all examples of physical capital. Like goods, we can touch physical capital. There is another kind of capital: human capital. Like services, human capital is intangible; it is not a physical object. Human capital includes all the things that we learn that help us produce more things in the future. The ability to read is human capital; it makes a person more productive than someone who does not have that ability. Human capital does not just come from formal education; it also includes things that we learn on the job or that we learn on our own.

When economists say resources are scarce, they do not mean it the same way as environmental pessimists who say that we are running out of trees, or water, or energy. Over time we can increase the amount of resources we have. We can increase our population, we can build more machines, and we can discover new natural resources. But at any single point in time there is only a certain amount of labor, natural resources, and capital available, so we have to make choices about how these resources are to be used.

Scarcity of resources is a problem because there are so many things that we value. For instance, many people value national defense, health care, art, entertainment, transportation, and leisure time. All of these things require resources to produce. Since we have only a certain amount of resources at any point in time, we have to choose among these things. If we want more of one thing, we have to give up some of something else. If we decide to use more of our resources for national defense because of terrorism, we have to reduce the resources used for production of health care, education, art, entertainment, or some other good.

SCARCITY MEANS THAT CHOICES HAVE COSTS

Every choice we make has a cost because we always have to give up one thing to get another. When I chose to spend an hour working on this book, I gave up an hour of playing with my kids. There are only so many hours in the day, and I cannot use the same hour for both. When I choose to go downtown and spend six dollars on a taco, I cannot spend the same six dollars on a hamburger at the restaurant next door. The value of what we give up to get something is its opportunity cost. Opportunity cost is much broader than what most people think of when they talk about cost. Usually when we ask what something costs, we get a price in dollars. But even things that do not cost money have a cost. When a person goes to college, the cost is not just the tuition and fees, it is also the money the person could have earned if they had gotten a job instead. Every choice has an opportunity cost because there is always something else that could have been done instead.

Opportunity cost is not the same for everyone. The opportunity cost of reading this book right now might be watching a television program, or it might be reading a novel, or it might be socializing with friends. The opportunity cost to you depends on what you would do instead.

> **Benjamin Franklin on Opportunity Cost**
>
> Economists did not invent opportunity cost, they just gave it a name. Ben Franklin emphasized the idea in his *Advice To Young Tradesmen* in 1748. On the opportunity cost of time he warned them, "Remember that time is money. He that can earn ten shillings a day and goes abroad or sits idle, one half of that day, though he spends only six pence during his diversion or idleness, ought not to reckon that the only expense: He has really spent, or thrown away, five shillings besides." On the opportunity cost of money he cautioned: "Remember that credit is money. If a man lets his money lie idle in my hands after it is due, he gives me the interest."

PEOPLE MAKE CHOICES RATIONALLY

Because choices always have costs, we generally do not make choices by flipping a coin or throwing darts. We weigh the costs and benefits and try to make the choices that we think will give us the greatest net benefit. The net benefit of a choice is the benefit gained minus the cost paid.

Most choices involve weighing the cost and benefits of doing something a little bit more or a little bit less. When you decide to buy a house or a car, it is not just a "yes" or only "no" question. Instead, you make choices about buying a little bit bigger house or a little bit better car, and you think about what you have to give up to get that little bit more. People tend to keep doing something as long as doing it a little bit more gives them more benefit than cost. Consider a student studying for an exam. The student starts studying for the exam because he believes that spending an hour studying gives greater benefit than his next-best alternative. Why does he eventually stop studying? He stops because after a while the cost of an additional hour of studying starts to outweigh the benefit.

Saying that each person tries to maximize his own net benefit is not the same as saying that people are all greedy and materialistic. A person may feel that she gets the greatest benefit by giving to others and choose to spend her time building a house with Habitat for Humanity rather than going on vacation. Most people tend to value a variety of things. They choose to consume houses and cars and vacations, but they also choose to go to church, to give to charity, and to participate in politics.

The combination of costs and benefits that influences a decision is called an incentive. People tend to respond in predictable ways to changes in incentives. If the cost of doing something increases, we do it less. If the benefit of doing something increases, we do it more. Businesses know that if they can lower the prices of their products, people will buy more. Legislators know that if they raise the tax on cigarettes, people will buy fewer cigarettes,

---

The Cost of Voting

As the cost of doing something increases, people do less of it. This idea is referred to as the law of demand. In markets, the law of demand means that when the price of a good rises, people buy less of it. The law of demand applies to nonmarket choices as well. In a study of voting in the Atlanta mayoral election in 2001, Moshe Haspel and Gibb Knotts found that voters who lived within a few blocks of a polling site were 10 percent more likely to vote than those who lived seven-tenths of a mile a way from their polling place. The higher the cost of voting, in terms of the time it took to get to a polling place, the less likely people were to vote.

---

and that if they give tax breaks for charitable giving, people will give more to charity.

Understanding the economy begins with understanding the problem of scarcity and how we respond to it as individuals, but it does not end there. Each person tries to make the choices that give him or her the greatest net benefit, but the economy is made up of many people, and they do not make their choices in isolation from each other. Instead, we all depend upon thousands of other people every day in order to obtain the goods and services we want to consume.

THE BENEFITS OF COOPERATION

The first thing I do in the morning is make a pot of coffee. Someone, probably in Africa, Asia, or Central America, grows and harvests the beans. Other people buy the beans, transport them, and roast them. The employees at the coffee shop put the beans on the shelf and sell them. I grind the beans in my coffee grinder (made in Mexico), place them in a filter, and pour in the water that I boiled in a copper kettle (made in China). I am only fifteen minutes into my day and already I have depended on the cooperation of dozens, if not hundreds, of people on four continents. Most of them do not know each other and none of them has any idea who I am, and yet they have all cooperated to provide me with a cup of coffee.

Most of us take this cooperation for granted, but about 250 years ago the Scottish philosopher Adam Smith recognized it as one of the greatest achievements of civilization. In 1776, Smith published his *Inquiry into the Nature and Causes of the Wealth of Nations*, and as a result he has come to be widely regarded as the founder of modern economics. Smith observed that, unlike people in the past, most people in modern economies produce very few of the goods they consume. We do not build our own shelter, raise our own food, or make our own clothes. Instead of being self-sufficient, spending our time doing many different things, we spend our time doing what we are good at. By practicing one thing, we get even better at it. Sometimes, because our attention is focused on one thing, we see better ways of doing it. Specialization enables us, as an economy, to produce far more goods and services than if each person tried to be self-sufficient. The problem is that to specialize in one thing, we have to get other people to make all the other things we want and then give them to us.

How do we get all these people to cooperate with us? If they are our friends or family, we might ask them to do it as a favor, but we do not know most of the people who make the goods we want to consume. We obtain their cooperation by appealing not to their good nature, but to their self-interest. We offer them something they want in exchange for something we want. This is what we do every time we go to a store. When we buy a candy bar, we are saying we would rather have it than the money; the owner of the store is saying she would rather have the money than the candy bar. So we trade. Each voluntary trade makes both sides, buyer and seller, better off than before.

It is intuitive to most people that specialization and trade can make people better off. What is not intuitive is that specialization and trade can make people better off even when one of them is not very good at anything.

Everyone Has a Comparative Advantage

People can always benefit from trade. To see why, consider a hypothetical example. Warren Buffett made a fortune of more than $40 billion by managing the investment firm Berkshire Hathaway. Now, imagine that Mr. Buffett is also the world's fastest typist. Should he do his own typing or hire someone who is slower than himself? He should hire a typist. The typist actually has an advantage over Warren Buffett when it comes to typing, even though he is slower. The typist's advantage is that spending an hour typing does not cost him nearly as much as it costs Mr. Buffett. The typist is not giving up millions of dollars that he could be earning by studying new investment opportunities.

A person who can do something at a lower cost than someone else has a comparative advantage at that thing. Everyone has a comparative advantage at something. The typist's comparative advantage does not come from being better at typing, it comes from the fact that Warren Buffett is so good at investment analysis. The better we are at something, the more costly it is for us *not* to do it, and the better off we will be if we can specialize and trade with others. In other words, the real benefit of trade is that it enables us to use our time and resources doing what we are relatively good at. The same benefits exist for trade between countries.

Specialization and trade are organized in different ways in different societies. Sometimes people specialize based on customs. In the past, a person was a farmer, or a weaver, or a blacksmith because his father was a farmer, or a weaver, or a blacksmith. Sometimes a government tells people what to produce and what trades they can and cannot make. In the Soviet Union there was a great deal of specialization and division of labor; the state told people what to specialize in and who they could sell it to.

In the United States we, as individuals, make most of the decisions about what we specialize in and with whom we trade. Almost 80 percent of all goods and services are produced by private businesses, and over 80 percent of the goods produced are purchased by households and businesses for consumption or investment. Several different names have been used to describe economies like the United States: a capitalist economy, a market economy, and a free enterprise system. All of these names mean essentially the same thing: Households and private businesses own the resources and make the decisions about how to allocate them. The decisions about what to produce, how to produce it, and who receives it are made by people voluntarily trading with each other in markets.

MARKETS ARE A FORM OF COOPERATION

Markets are where people come together to buy and sell. There are many different types of markets. In the past, markets were often located in a specific place. In some old towns it is still possible to locate the original market square. Now many of the markets that people use do not have a physical location. You may hear reports on the news about what is happening to stocks on Nasdaq, but no one can tell you where Nasdaq is, because it does not exist in a specific location. Nasdaq is the National Association of Securities Dealers Automated Quotation system, and it is composed of securities dealers all over the country connected by an electronic network.

Some markets are quite small, such as a farmers' market in a small town. Other markets are fairly large. The market for homes in cities usually extends well beyond the city limits. For example, it is not unusual for people who work in Washington, D.C., to live as far as fifty miles away from the city. Some markets, such as the market for crude oil, encompass the entire world. The price of oil is determined not just by people in the United States, but by people all over the world buying and selling oil.

Adam Smith saw in the competition of the marketplace a type of co-operation that was not directed by anyone, but that instead emerged from each person trying to do the best he could for himself. As a result of participation in markets, people get the goods and services they want at the lowest possible price. If a seller does not provide people with what they want, the seller goes out of business. If a seller tries to charge too high a price, a second seller makes a nice profit by undercutting her and stealing her customers. According to Smith, each person trying to achieve her own personal gain is led as if by an "invisible hand" to produce the most benefit for society.

Supply and Demand: How Markets Work

The price of a good or service in a market is determined by the actions of both buyers and sellers. In other words, price is determined by supply and demand. It has been said that if a person teaches a parrot to say "supply and demand," he will have created an economist, and sometimes it seems like that is not far from the truth. If we want to know why the price of gas goes up, the answer is found in changes in the supply and demand for gas. If we want to know why more homes have computers, the answer is found in

A farmer's market is one of many types of markets in which goods and services are exchanged. Corbis.

changes in the supply and demand for computers. In a market economy, anytime we want to understand what gets produced and why it costs what it does, we look at supply and demand.

Demand is the quantity of a good or service that buyers plan to purchase. Demand is not a wish list. Buyers have to be both willing and able to make the purchase. Supply is the quantity that suppliers plan to sell. Again, supply is not a wish list, but it is what sellers are actually willing and able to do. Like any plans, supply and demand are not written in stone. When we make plans, they are conditional upon certain other things not changing. We may plan to go hiking this weekend, as long as it does not rain. We may plan to put two hundred dollars in our saving account this month, as long as we do not have any unexpected car repairs. Our plans about buying and selling also depend on certain other things not changing.

Things That Influence Demand

The list of important things that influence how much we plan to buy is relatively short. The important things include: the price of the good, income and wealth, the price of substitutes for the good, the price of things that we consume along with the good, tastes, expectations about the future, and the population.

The Price of the Good. As the price of a good falls, the quantity we plan to purchase goes up. Imagine the average price of CDs is $20. How many CDs would you plan to buy in a month? Now imagine the price is $15, then $10, then $5. What happens to the quantity of CDs you would plan to buy as the price falls? Most people would plan to purchase more at the lower prices. There are two reasons why people plan to purchase more at lower prices. First, they can afford to buy more at lower prices. If you budgeted $40 for CDs, that $40 will buy eight CDs at $5 apiece, but only two at $20 apiece. Second, at the higher prices, buyers are more likely to choose to purchase substitutes for the good. At the higher CD prices, people are more likely to download songs from the Internet or spend the money on some other form of entertainment.

Even if you as an individual do not buy more as the price falls, the market demand still increases as the price falls because people have different preferences. Some people are willing to pay a lot for a CD, but others are willing to pay only a little. At high prices, only the people who are willing to pay a lot plan to buy. At low prices, those people still plan to purchase CDs, and the people who are willing to spend only a little join them.

Income and Wealth. Consider the CD example again, but now imagine that you have just won $10 million in the lottery. Would your answers to the question of how many CDs do you plan to buy each month be the same? Chances are that at any of those prices you would plan to buy more than you had before. What if you lost your job? Would you plan to buy as many as before? Probably not. For many goods, we expect that as income goes up, we will plan to buy more. There are some goods, however, that many people plan to buy less of as their income goes up. Some college students practically live on ramen noodles and macaroni and cheese. Most of them buy less ramen noodles and macaroni and cheese after they graduate and get a job.

The Prices of Substitutes for the Good. Recently the number of CDs purchased has been declining. This may be associated with the price of a related good. CDs and downloaded music are related to each other; they are substitutes. The cost of downloading music over the Internet has been falling as the price of computers has fallen and access to the Internet has expanded. As the substitute for CDs becomes cheaper, people consume more of the substitute and less of the CDs.

The more closely one thing is regarded as a substitute for another, the more their prices are related. Two things that are regarded as exactly the same are perfect substitutes and should have the same price.

The Prices of Things Consumed along with The Good. The demand for DVDs increased as the price of DVD players fell. DVDs and DVD players are examples of goods that are consumed together. Many goods are consumed only in combination with each other: gas and cars, computers and software, lamps and lightbulbs. What is happening in the market for one can influence what is happening in the market for the other.

Tastes. Recently, many stores have begun to carry organic foods, grown without pesticides or herbicides. The reason is a change in tastes. Many people have been persuaded that such foods are healthier or better tasting. People's basic tastes tend to be pretty stable: We like food, shelter, clothing, and entertainment. But how we choose to satisfy those basic tastes is constantly evolving.

Expectations. Sometimes demand is driven largely by what people expect to happen to the price in the future. Sometimes people are more willing to buy homes or stocks if they think their price is going to rise in the future. This can lead to a self-fulfilling prophecy. People think that the price will go up, so they buy. Their buying helps drive the price up. Other people see the price going up and want to get in on the action, so the price goes up even more.

Population. The more buyers in a market, the greater the demand is. Housing prices in northern Virginia increased rapidly during the early 2000s. Part of this increase was attributable to the fact that the several counties had rates of population growth that were among the highest in the country.

Things That Influence Supply

The list of things that influence supply is relatively short. The things that are important to sellers are all about the relationship between the price of the good and the cost of producing it. The things that are important to suppliers are: the price of the good or service to be sold, the prices of resources needed to produce the good or service, the technology available to produce the good or service, and the number of sellers.

The Price of the Good. The quantity of a good that a business plans to sell increases as the price increases. Just as buyers do not all have the same preferences, sellers do not all have the same costs of production. Some sellers can produce at a very low cost, others can produce only at a high cost. At a low price, only the low-cost firms can afford to produce and sell. At a high price, the high-cost firms are also willing to sell, but the low-cost firms are still willing to sell as well.

The Cost of the Resources Needed to Make the Good. The quantity that sellers plan to provide changes as the costs of production change. If the price of gold increases, jewelers have higher costs than they did before the price increased. The lowest price any jeweler can accept will be higher than it was before.

The Technology Available for Making the Good. When a business develops a new technique that enables it to produce at a lower cost, it is able to increase the supply of the good. For example, the introduction of the automated assembly line dramatically lowered the cost of producing automobiles, increased the supply, and lowered the price.

The Number of Sellers. The more sellers there are in a market, the greater is the supply at any particular price.

Supply and Demand Curves

Supply and demand are often represented visually, as in Figures 1.1 and 1.2. Although you may never see a supply-and-demand graph unless you take a course in economics, it's a good idea to know what they look like, because they form the foundation for the understanding of markets. When you read in a newspaper or a magazine about why the price of something is rising or falling, the writer almost certainly is thinking in terms of supply and demand.

Figure 1.1 shows demand. All the possible prices of the good are shown on the vertical axis. Quantities of the good are shown on the horizontal axis. The downward sloping line, called a demand curve, shows the relationship between the price of the good and the quantity of the good people plan to purchase. It shows how plans change as the price of the good changes. A demand curve is drawn with the assumption that the price of the good is the only thing that changes. All of the other things that matter to people stay the same. If nothing else changes, people plan to buy more of a good as the price of that good falls.

If one of the other important things changes, then people's plans change. To show this change visually, we draw a new demand curve. For instance, if someone won the lottery, he would plan to buy more than before at any

FIGURE 1.1
Demand Shifts

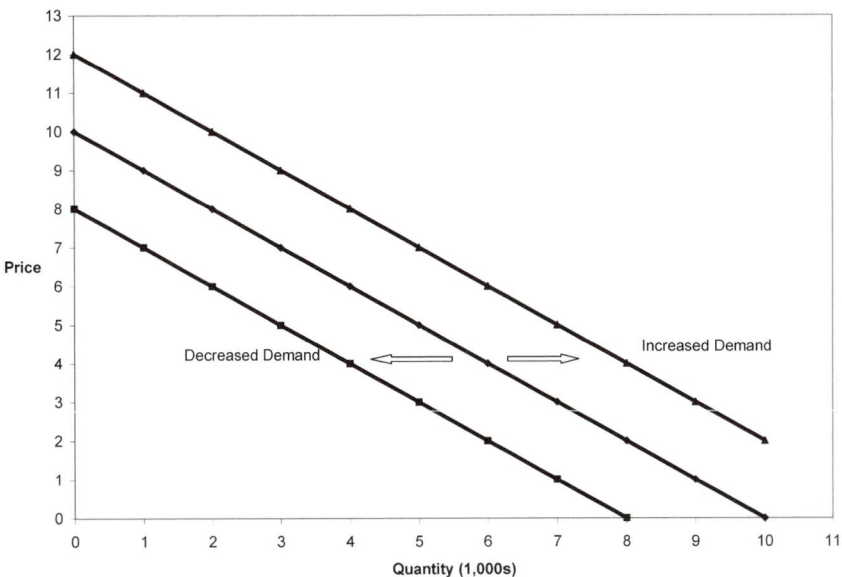

FIGURE 1.2
Supply Shifts

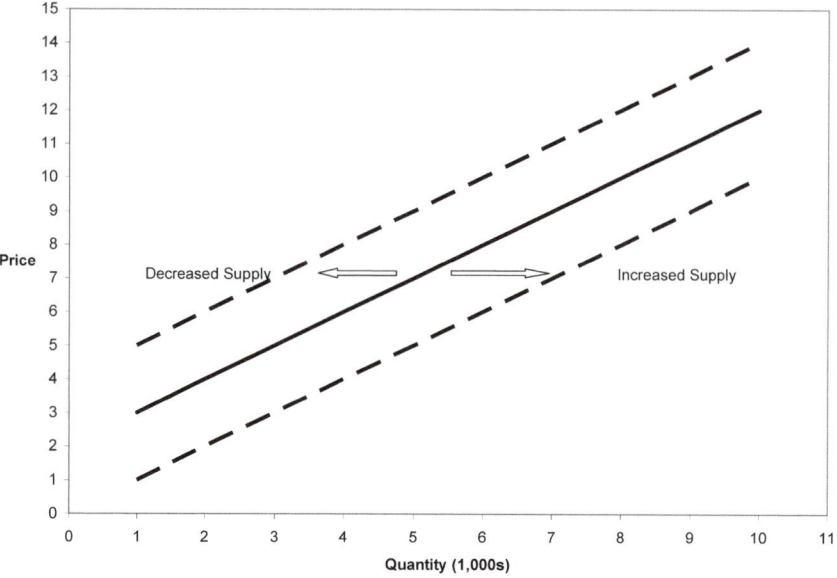

Quantity (1,000s)

price. We show this increase in demand with a curve that is further out to the right. If something happens that makes people less willing to buy at any price, then we show this decrease in demand with a curve that is further in to the left.

The supply curve in Figure 1.2 slopes up from left to right, showing that businesses plan to produce more at high prices than at low prices. If one of the other things that is important to sellers changes their plans change, and we draw a new supply curve. If something happens that makes them plan to offer more than before at any price, then we draw a supply curve that is further out to the right. If something happens that makes suppliers plan to offer less at any price, we draw a supply curve that is further in to the left.

The graph makes it easy to see how supply and demand interact with each other to determine the price and the quantity sold. Figure 1.3 shows both supply and demand. We expect 5,000 units to be sold at a price of $5 each. To see why, consider what would happen if the price is not $5. At a price of $8, suppliers want to sell 8,000, but buyers want to purchase only 2,000. The plans of the buyers and the sellers do not mesh at that price. There is a surplus of the good. Suppliers find the good piling up on their shelves. Since their plans did not work out the way they wanted, sellers have an incentive

FIGURE 1.3
Supply and Demand

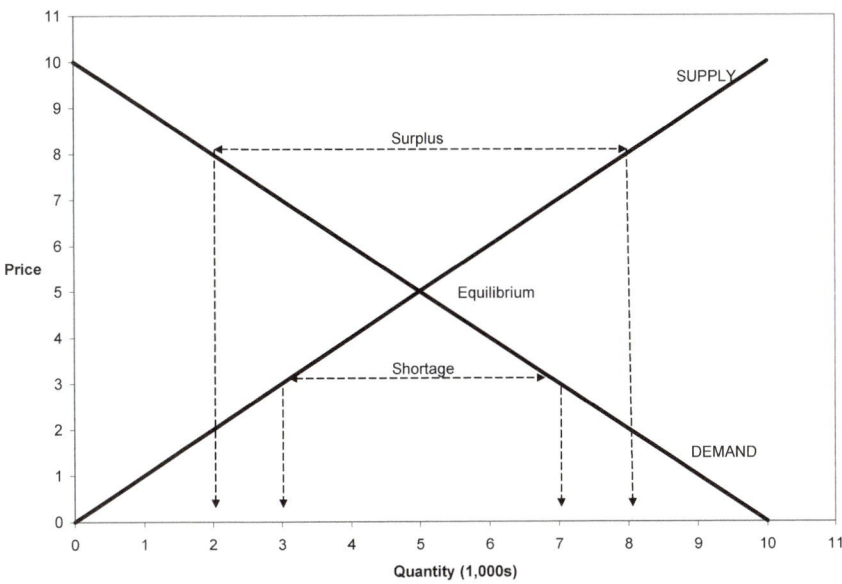

Quantity (1,000s)

to change what they are doing. They lower the price and reduce their production to get rid of the surplus. The price and the quantity move toward $5 and 5,000.

At a price of $3, buyers would like to purchase 7,000, but suppliers are willing to provide only 3,000. There is a shortage of the good at $3. Businesses have to turn away people who want to buy. Again their plans did not work out the way they thought they would, and there is an incentive to change. Suppliers raise their prices and increase production to get rid of the shortage. The price and quantity move toward $5 and 5,000.

Now think about what happens at a price of $5. At $5, buyers plan to purchase 5,000 and sellers plan to unload 5,000. Everything works out as planned. There is no incentive to change. The intersection of supply and demand shown in Figure 1.3 is called the equilibrium. The equilibrium price is the one we expect to see because it is the only price at which all of the buyers' plans and all of the sellers' plans work out as expected. Again, at the intersection of supply and demand there is no incentive for either buyers or sellers to change what they are doing. For the price to change, either the supply curve or the demand curve has to change. For the supply curve or the demand curve to change, something other than the price of the good has to change.

Applying Supply and Demand

In 2005, many states cut back on road repair. The reason for the cutbacks was the escalating cost of road work. If the cost of production increases, the supply curve moves to the left. The new equilibrium is at a higher price and at a lower quantity than before. The causes of the higher cost of road work were increasing costs of asphalt and fuel for equipment. On average, the price of asphalt had risen 13 percent from the previous year. Behind this increase in price was yet another increase in the cost of production. Asphalt is derived from crude oil, and the price of crude oil had risen 75 percent over the previous two years.

As of 2004, retail prices of organic milk were rising by about 20 percent a year. When a change in tastes causes an increase in demand, the demand curve moves out to the right, and we expect both the price of the good and the quantity that is sold to increase. In recent years organic milk has seen just such an increase in demand. Many people have decided that they would like to get milk from cows that were not given antibiotics or hormones to increase their production.

By 1913, Henry Ford had been building automobiles for over a decade. Ford had focused on lowering costs by using standardized parts. Some of his employees got the idea that he could increase productivity by having workers stay in place and specialize in one part of the production process as the cars moved past them on an automated assembly line. They were right. In 1913, it took 12.5 hours to assemble a Model T; in 1914 it took 1.5 hours. The price of the Model T dropped from $600 in 1912 to $440 in 1920, and to $290 in 1924. When changes in technology lower the cost of production, the supply curve shifts to the right. The price falls and the quantity sold increases.

Shifts in supply and demand cause not only the rise and fall of prices, but the rise and fall of companies and entire industries. When demand falls, prices and profits fall. As profits fall, some sellers decide they would be better off doing something else. The number of sellers decreases, and resources flow toward some other market where they are more highly valued. When demand for a product increases, prices and profits rise. The high profits attract new sellers to the industry. The number of suppliers increases, and a larger share of society's resources (land, labor, and capital) flow into the market. Thus we can consider the more long-term consequences of our examples.

In 2004, the largest supplier of crude oil to the United States was Canada. High oil prices led Canadian companies to develop methods of extracting oil from "tar sands." As the price of oil increases, more resources flow toward the production of oil as well as the production of goods that can substitute for oil. Rather than looking for pools of crude oil below the ground, the

Canadian oil companies looked for places where oil is mixed in with the soil. They developed methods to extract the oil from the sand. Improvements in technology have lowered the cost of production from tar sands to the point where it would be profitable to mine oil from tar sands even if the price of oil fell as low as $20 a barrel.

The Northeast Organic Dairy Producers Alliance reported that there was a 370 percent increase in the number of organic dairy cows between 1997 and 2001. Between 1990 and 2003 the number of organic dairy farms in Vermont increased from three to sixty while the number of conventional farms fell from more than 2,000 to 1,400. Over time, as people switched from regular milk to organic milk, resources were shifted from regular dairy production to organic production. Conventional farms still outnumber organic farms by a long way, but resources (land, natural resources, and capital) are flowing toward the organic market in response to an increase in demand.

As the price of Models Ts fell, Ford's sales and its share of the automobile market increased. In 1911, Ford sold 40,000 cars. In 1917, it sold 741,000. In the early 1920s, Ford was producing about half of all the cars made in the world. Ford was able to attract resources away from other automobile manufacturers. In 1916, Ford raised the daily wage to $5.00 a day, twice the going rate. Ford's ability to use resources more productively than other automobile producers meant that Ford was able to draw resources to itself by paying a higher price for them.

THE CIRCULAR FLOW OF THE AMERICAN ECONOMY

Just as markets are made up of many people buying and selling, the economy is made up of many markets. Figure 1.4 shows how all the different parts of the economy are connected to each other by markets. Economists call Figure 1.4 a circular flow diagram. The circular flow diagram divides the people in the economy into four groups, or sectors: business, households, government, and the international sector. The four sectors are not composed of different people; instead they describe different things that people do. The same person who makes business decisions all day makes household decisions at night and influences government decisions when she votes. All of the people in the economy are connected to each other by markets: markets for resources, markets for goods and services, and financial markets.

The basic circular flow of the economy is established by households and businesses. When they are connected by markets for resources and markets for goods and services, a circle is formed. The circle emphasizes how the different parts of the economy are influenced by each other. People in households sell resources to businesses. Mostly what households sell to businesses is labor.

FIGURE 1.4
The Circular Flow of a Market Economy

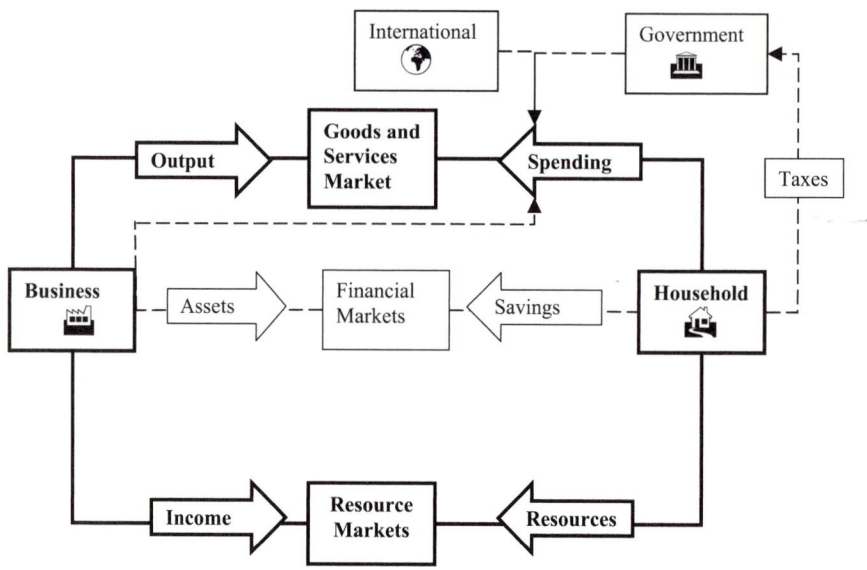

Businesses buy resources from households and produce goods and services to sell. Households buy the goods and services that businesses produce. The more households buy, the more revenue the businesses get. The more revenue the businesses get, the more income the households receive. The more income households receive, the more goods they buy.

Households also save part of the income they earn. They put their savings into savings accounts, checking accounts, certificates of deposit, mutual funds, and other assets. Their savings can then be used by businesses to finance investment.

People in other countries, the international sector, enter the market for goods and services through imports and exports. In addition, they can enter financial markets as borrowers or lenders. Government enters the circular flow through taxes, purchases of goods and services, and borrowing and lending in financial markets. Through government, people also enact the laws that regulate economic activity.

THE ROLE OF MONEY IN THE AMERICAN ECONOMY

In the circular flow diagram, the different parts of the economy are connected by flows in each direction. One flow is moving clockwise; it is a flow of things. Goods and services flow out of businesses toward households, government, foreigners, and other businesses. Resources flow out of households and toward businesses. The other flow moves counterclockwise. It is a flow of monetary payments. Wages, salaries, rent, interest, and profit flow from businesses to households. Payments for goods and services flow from households, government, foreigners, and businesses to businesses.

Many people think that money is what economics is all about. Money, however, is really just a tool that we use to make it easier to trade resources for goods and services. Without money, people could still specialize and engage in division of labor, but it would be more difficult. You could trade with people only when you had something they wanted and they had something you wanted. That is, you would have to resort to barter.

Money gets rid of the problem of barter. The defining characteristic of money is that it is a medium of exchange. Medium of exchange is just a fancy way of saying that we can always use money to pay for something. Anyone who is selling something will be happy to take money in payment, because she knows she can use that money to buy whatever it is that she wants.

A lot of different things have been used as money. In the prisoner-of-war camps during World War II, soldiers used cigarettes for money. In colonial Virginia, settlers used tobacco for money. Other people, in other times and places, have used things such as shells, stones, and cattle for money. One of the great things about money is that people did not even have to try to invent it. Whenever there was something that everyone wanted, it became money. Because everyone wanted it, people could always use it to pay for things. In many places, people eventually came to use precious metals like gold and silver as money. Everyone wanted these precious metals. In addition, metals do not die, they do not rot, and they cannot be smoked. In addition, they were scarce, and even small amounts were very valuable, so people did not usually have to carry around large amounts.

In the United States, both gold and silver were money during the nineteenth century. That does not mean that people always carried gold and silver to pay for things. People put their gold and silver money in banks for safekeeping. The banks issued banknotes that could be exchanged between people, and then taken back to the bank and exchanged for gold and silver. As long as people trusted the bank to give them gold or silver in exchange for the notes, the notes were as good as gold, and people could use them as money.

Today we still use banknotes as money. Dollars are Federal Reserve Notes. Two things are different about our banknotes today. First, all of our notes today come from the same bank, the Federal Reserve. Second, gold and silver are not money anymore; they have not been since 1933. Federal Reserve Notes are not backed by anything more than the government's

TABLE 1.1
The Money Supply (M1), March 2005 (billion $)

Currency	$703.9
Travelers Checks	7.5
Demand Deposits	660.1
Total M1	1371.5

Source: Federal Reserve Board, Statistics: Releases and Historical Data;
http://www.federalreserve.gov/releases/

declaration that they are money and our faith that people will take them. Such currencies are called fiat currencies.

In addition to Federal Reserve Notes, we use coins, travelers checks, and checking accounts. These are the things that we can go into a store and spend. Table 1.1 shows the different parts of the money supply. The largest parts are currency and checkable deposits, the money that people have in their checking accounts.

Many people pay for most things with a credit card. But credit cards are not money because when you use your credit cards, you are not actually paying for something—on your receipt you sign that you agree to pay for it later, when the credit card bill comes. Credit cards are a means of postponing payment rather than a means of payment.

There are other things that are nearly money: savings accounts, certificates of deposit, money market accounts. If you ask a person how much money they have, they would very likely include these things. The difference between this second group of financial assets and the first group is that these are not things that we can take directly into a store and spend. We first have to take some step to convert these assets into something we can spend. For instance, to spend what is in your savings account, you either have to make a withdrawal, converting the savings into Federal Reserve Notes, or you have to transfer the money to your checking account.

Because some things are money and other things are very nearly money, the government has several measures of the money supply. The first and most narrow is called M1, which includes only those things that can be spent directly: coins, currency, travelers checks, and checking accounts. Next is M2, which includes everything that is in M1 and then adds things that are nearly money. There is also an M3 that includes everything in M2 and adds things that are even more difficult to convert into a medium of exchange.

People often think that more money is always better, but money and wealth are not the same. Money is only a part of wealth, which also includes real estate, stocks, bonds, and other valuable items. Demand for wealth may be limitless, but the demand for money is limited to our need to use it. A person who inherits $10 million is unlikely to leave all of it as money in a checking account. He spends some of it, buying a new house, a new car, or some new clothes. He does not want to leave it all in a checking account because the rate of return is not very high. Certificates of deposit have higher rates of interest; so do bonds and stocks. In other words, he takes most of the money and turns it into things that are not money.

Another way to see that money is just a tool is to recognize that each dollar is used many times. When we spend a dollar at a store, it goes into the cash register and may be given to someone else as change. That person spends it somewhere else. The average number of times a dollar is spent to buy part of our Gross Domestic Product is called the velocity of money because it describes how quickly the money is moving from person to person.

Because money is just a tool that we use to buy goods and services, we cannot increase the amount of goods in the economy just by printing more money. The amount of goods we can produce is determined by our resources and technology. So if the Federal Reserve creates more money but the amount of goods stays the same, all we will be able to do is bid up the price of goods. Money is important and we will give much more attention to its role in the economy, especially when it comes to business cycles, but in the end it is just a tool. Like other tools, it can work well or work poorly, but we are not ultimately interested in that. In the end, the wealth of a nation is the amount of goods and services available to its people.

Two

Measuring the Performance
of the American Economy

The British politician Benjamin Disraeli once declared that there are three kinds of lies: "Lies, damn lies, and statistics." To avoid being lied to with economic statistics, it is necessary to understand how economic performance is measured.

It is easy to measure what is happening in a particular market. The price of gas at the station around the corner from my house is $2.09 today. Measuring the performance of the entire economy is not as straightforward because we are looking at millions of different goods and services. The objective of this chapter is to provide an introduction to how production, employment, and prices are measured for the economy as a whole.

MEASURING TOTAL PRODUCTION

Measuring the total production of an economy is called national income and product accounting. In the United States, the Bureau of Economic Analysis of the Commerce Department is responsible for national income and product accounts. They are called income and product accounts because in a market economy we can measure the total amount of production either by counting the flow of payments in the market for goods and services produced or by counting the flow of income in the market for resources. Total production and total income have to be nearly equal because there are two sides to every sale. Every payment by a buyer is income to a seller. The total amount of production is the Gross Domestic Product (GDP), and the total amount of income is national income.

Measuring Gross Domestic Product

The most widely used measure of economic performance is GDP. In 2003 the GDP of the United States was $10,987,900,000,000. That is, GDP was more than $10 trillion. GDP is defined as the *market value* of *final* goods and services produced *in a country* during *a specific period of time*. Each part of the definition is important.

To say that GDP is the market value of goods and services means that we use the market prices of goods when we add them up. If a particular car costs $12,000 in 2003 and there are 10,000 produced in that year, that production adds $120 million to GDP for 2003. Using market prices gives the same importance to each good that buyers give it. If buyers say that each unit of one good is worth twice as much as each unit of another, then each unit of that good counts twice as much in GDP as well.

When we use the market prices that existed during a year to calculate GDP during that year, we have an estimate of nominal GDP, also called GDP in current dollars. The problem with nominal GDP is that prices can change even when production does not. If the exact same car that sold for

Manufacturing production is one of the key components of the Gross Domestic Product. Getty Images: John A. Rizzo.

$12,000 in 2003 sells for $13,000 in 2004, and we again produce 10,000 cars, the production of those cars now adds $130 million to GDP. It looks like production had increased when in fact it had not.

To get around the problem of changing prices, we keep using the same year's market prices year after year. For instance, we could use the prices that existed in 1997. When we use the prices that existed in another year to value GDP, the result is called real GDP. If we use 1997 prices, then we say that we have measured real GDP in 1997 dollars. If we use the 1997 price for both years, then producing 10,000 cars in 2003 would add $10 million to real GDP in 2003, and producing 10,000 cars again in 2004 would again add $10 million to real GDP. Using the 1997 prices eliminates the effect of changes in prices. Real GDP increases only when the amount of goods and services produced actually increases.

Real GDP is not real in any absolute sense. "Real" indicates that we are measuring things in terms of the prices that existed in a specific year. You can have real GDP in 1971 dollars, or 1985 dollars, or 1997 dollars, or any other year's dollars that you want, but you need to specify what the year is. References to real dollars, real GDP, or real wages are meaningless if the base year is not stated.

Since 1996 the Bureau of Economic Analysis has used a more complicated procedure to calculate real GDP. The procedure allows the relative importance of different goods and their prices to change each year as they actually do in the economy. The resulting estimates are referred to as chain weighted. When the BEA reports real GDP, it is in chained $s. Figure 2.1 shows the growth of real GDP (in chained 1996 $s) from 1929 to 2002. The process necessary to create chain weighted estimates is much more complicated than simply using the prices from a prior year, but the objective is the same, to remove the effects of inflation from our estimates of production and income.

The phrase *final goods* reminds us that we need to be careful not to count goods twice. For example, if a furniture manufacturer buys $1,000 worth of lumber from a lumber mill and then produces tables that are sold for $2,000, we count only the $2,000 table, the final good, as part of GDP. If we count both the $1,000 of lumber and the $2,000 table, we are counting the lumber twice because its value is included in the value of the table.

The phrase *within a country* distinguishes Gross Domestic Product from a similar measure called Gross National Product. Gross Domestic Product measures the production within a country regardless of who does it. Gross National Product measures the production of a country's citizens regardless of where they are located. GDP is now the measure most commonly used in the United States, but you may still find some comparative data that refers

FIGURE 2.1
Real Per Capita GDP in (chained) 1996 dollars, 1929–2002

Source: Mini Historical Statistics, HS–33. Selected Per Capita Income and Product Items in Current and Real (1996) Dollars: 1929 to 2002, http://www.census.gov/statab/www/minihs.html

to GNP. It does not really make much difference which is used. For the United States, GNP is about 0.3 percent higher than GDP.

The last part of the definition of GDP states that we are measuring the production over *a specific period of time.* The goods and services produced in a year do not exist at a single point in time, such as at the end of the year. Many services disappear as they are consumed. We say that GDP is a flow variable rather than a stock variable. The amount of water in a bathtub is stock variable, but a shower is measured by its flow, the amount of water that flows through it in a certain amount of time. Flow variables like GDP can be measured only over a specific period of time.

The same sectors of the economy used in the circular flow diagram (Figure 1.4) are used in national income accounting. Table 2.1 shows nominal GDP for 2003. GDP is divided into four categories based upon who the buyer is, in the market for goods and services: household consumption expenditures, business investment, government expenditures, and net exports.

The names of the categories used in GDP do not mean exactly the same thing in national income accounting that they do when people use them in everyday conversation. For example, the largest item listed in Table 2.1 is

TABLE 2.1
Nominal U.S. GDP and Its Components, 2003 (billion $)

Gross Domestic Product	11,004.1
Personal consumption expenditures	7,760.9
Gross private domestic investment	1,665.8
Net exports of goods and services	−498.1
Government consumption expenditures and gross investment	2075.5

Source: Economic Report of the President, 2005. Table B-1, Gross Domestic Product, 1959–2004.

household consumption expenditure. This sounds like all the spending that households do during the year. It isn't. The only spending that is counted in GDP is spending for things produced in 2003. If a household buys a used car, that spending is not counted in GDP because the car was not produced during this year. The car was counted as part of GDP in the year that it was produced.

Government expenditures also sound like they should count everything that the government spends, but here again national income accounting counts only government spending that goes to purchase goods and services produced in the current year. A large part of the federal government's budget does not fall into that category. Payments that go to people, but do not buy any good or service from them, are called transfer payments, and they are not counted as part of government expenditures in GDP. To know whether some part of the government budget is counted in GDP, we ask, "Did it buy something produced this year?" Are Social Security payments part of GDP? No; they didn't buy anything. What about unemployment benefits? No; they didn't buy anything. What about President Bush's salary? Yes; we purchased his services as president for the year. The same thing goes for state and local budgets. Their spending is counted as part of government expenditures only when it goes to purchase a good or service produced this year.

Investment also means something different in national income accounting than it means in ordinary conversation. In national income accounting, investment spending counts purchases of newly produced equipment, software, and buildings (known as capital) by businesses. In ordinary conversation, when people say "investment," they often mean activities in the stock market, but investment spending as part of GDP does not include purchases of stocks. A share of stock is not a good or a service. Stocks represent ownership in a company. If you own stock in a corporation, you are a part owner. Buying and selling stock is like buying a used car. In both cases, people transfer ownership of something that already exists; they do not produce something new.

There are two other confusing issues with the use of the term "investment" in GDP: residential construction and inventories. Residential construction is building new homes. Many people would regard a newly constructed home as expenditure by a household, but in national income accounting it is counted as part of investment. Investment also includes changes in inventories from the beginning of the year to its end. Inventories are goods that businesses have in stock. There are inventories of inputs and inventories of outputs. For example, a computer manufacturer probably has some finished computers ready to ship when orders come in, and they have computer chips and other parts on hand for construction of more computers.

We can also ask if certain things fall into the category of investment. Is the purchase of one hundred shares of Microsoft investment? No; it did not buy a good or service. What if the restaurant Soup 'n Taco buys a new computer to keep records on? Yes; it bought a newly produced good in order to help it produce more in the future. Your grandma buys a savings bond for your birthday? No; it didn't buy a good. Your parents have a new house built? Yes; it is residential construction. Circuit City experiences an increase in its inventories because sales were lower than expected? Yes; they bought newly produced goods.

MEASURING NATIONAL INCOME

The other side of the circular flow of the economy is income. Table 2.2 shows nominal national income for 2003. The terms used in national income are more like what we use in everyday conversation: employee compensation, rental income, proprietors' income, and corporate profits. Employee compensation includes wages and salaries, plus contributions to

TABLE 2.2
Nominal National Income and Its Components, 2003 (billion $)

National Income	9679
Employees' Compensation	6289
Proprietors' Income	834.1
Corporate Profits	1021.1
Rental Income	153.8
Net Interest	543
Gov't. Taxes on Production and Imports, Transfers to Businesses, and Surplus of Gov't. Enterprises	838

Source: Economic Report of the President, 2005. Table B-28, national income by type of income, 1959–2004.

government social insurance plans, plus contributions to private pension and insurance plans.

Gross Domestic Product and national income have to be very nearly the same but not exactly the same. In 2003, national income was about $1.3 trillion less than Gross Domestic Product. Table 2.3 shows how we get from GDP to national income. First, GDP counts only the income generated in the United States. If you own a factory in another country, the production does not take place here but you may still receive income from it. So we add income that Americans get from owning things in other countries and subtract the income paid to people in other countries. After we make this adjustment, we have Gross National Product (GNP); it is really not much different from GDP. The big difference between GDP and national income arises from Consumption of Fixed Capital. Consumption of Fixed Capital (also known as depreciation) refers to the fact that when we use equipment and buildings, they wear out. Part of national production each year needs to go to replacing these things as they wear out. The last adjustment is Statistical Discrepancy, which is a way of saying nobody is perfect. If you have two people measure something from different angles, there is a good chance that they won't come up with exactly the same number. As a percentage of GDP, this statistical discrepancy is very small, less than one-quarter of 1 percent.

Other measures of income can be derived from national income. Personal income equals national income minus contributions to government social insurance programs. Disposable personal income equals personal income minus taxes and interest payments. Disposable personal income is of particular interest because it reflects the amount of income that households actually have available to save or to buy goods and services.

TABLE 2.3
Reconciling Nominal GDP and Nominal National Income in 2003 (billion $)

Gross domestic product	11,004.0
Plus: Income receipts from rest of the world	329.0
Less: Income payments to rest of the world	−273.9
Equals: Gross national product	11,059.1
Less: Consumption of fixed capital	−1,353.9
Equals: Net national product	9,705.2
Less: Statistical discrepancy	−25.6
Equals: National income	9,679.6

Source: Economic Report of the President, 2005. Table B-26, relation of Gross Domestic Product, Gross National Product, net national product, and national income, 1959–2004.

PER CAPITA MEASURES OF PRODUCTION AND PRODUCTIVITY

Per capita GDP or per capita income tell us even more about how the economy is doing than total GDP or income. Per capita GDP is the total GDP divided by the population. A country with a large population, like India, can have a large GDP but a small per capita GDP. The countries that are regarded as wealthy are ones with large per capita GDP. We really want to know how much in goods and services the average person has. But even per capita GDP can be misleading in terms of examining a nation's standard of living. For example, we can increase the per capita GDP by having more people work or by having people work longer each year (by taking less vacation or by working longer hours).

A measure of production similar to per capita GDP is productivity. Productivity divides total output by the inputs used to produce it. It is possible to divide output by any one of the inputs used to produce it or by all of them together. Labor productivity is total output divided by the amount of labor input used to produce it. Total factor productivity is total output divided by all of the inputs used to produce it. Increases in total factor productivity indicate improvements in the use of all resources combined.

Increased productivity is the key to economic progress. In the long run, the only way the average person can consume more is if the average person produces more.

Calculating Growth Rates

The rate of growth of any of the measures of production is calculated as the percentage change since the previous year. Percentage change is the difference between the value of the variable in year 1 and the value of the variable in year 2 divided by the value in year 1. For instance, in 2002, nominal GDP in the United States was $10,487 billion, and in 2003 it was $11,004 billion. To calculate the rate of growth, first find the change in GDP. The change from year 1 to year 2 was $11,004 − $10,487 = $517 billion. Then divide the change by the level of GDP in year 1:

$517 billion ÷ $10,487 billion = .049.

This result can be multiplied by 100 to express it in percentage form. Thus nominal GDP in 2003 was 4.9 percent higher than in 2002. A rate of growth of 4.9 percent a year would lead to a doubling of GDP in about fourteen years if it continued. To calculate the growth in real GDP, we would simply use the values for real GDP in each year.

MEASURING LABOR AND EMPLOYMENT

In general, an increase in GDP is associated with an increase in employment; a decrease in GDP is associated with an increase in unemployment. Figure 2.2 shows how we measure employment and unemployment among people in the economy. The largest circle represents the entire population. The next-largest circle represents the part of the population that is of working age (16–65). Some of the people in the working-age population are in the labor force, but some are not in the labor force. The labor force includes all the people who are employed and all of the people who are actively seeking employment. The rate of unemployment is the percentage of the labor force that is not employed. The labor force does not include people who live in institutions such as prisons or hospitals, nor does it include military personnel on active duty.

The government does not actually count each unemployed person. Each month the Bureau of Labor Statistics surveys 60,000 households. Unemployment statistics are based on this sample. Each person in the surveyed household is classified as not in the labor force, employed, or unemployed. The unemployment rate does not account for how much people are working. If a person has a job, he is counted as employed even if the job is part-time. Because of the survey method of measurement, the unemployment rate is

FIGURE 2.2
Labor Force and Unemployment

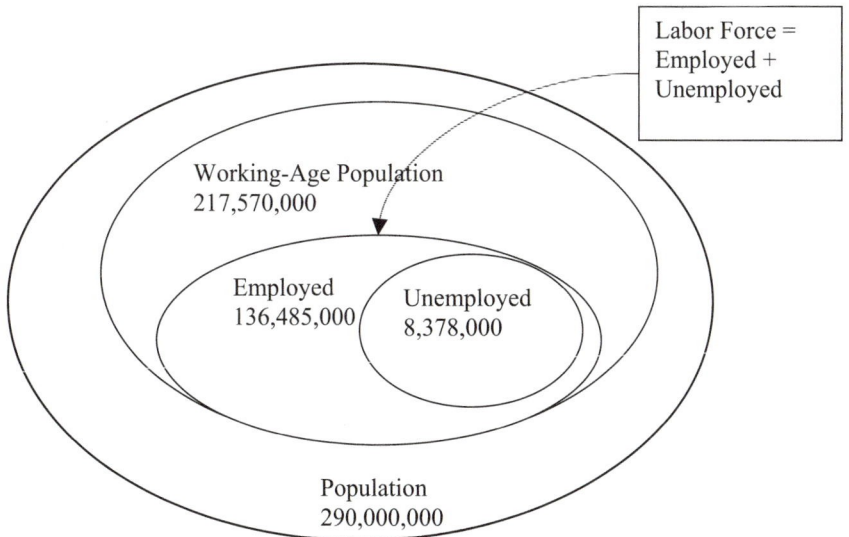

Labor Force =
Employed +
Unemployed

Working-Age Population
217,570,000

Employed
136,485,000

Unemployed
8,378,000

Population
290,000,000

Calculating the Unemployment Rate

The labor force and the unemployment rate are calculated as follows:

Labor force = number of employed + number of unemployed

Unemployment rate = Number of unemployed ÷ Labor Force

In 2003, there were 146,510,000 people in the labor force; 137,736,000 of them were employed and 8,774,000 of them were unemployed. The unemployment rate in 2003 was

8,774,000 ÷ 146,510,000 = .059

Multiplying by 100, we can express this as 5.9 percent.

---

influenced by discouraged and encouraged workers. During a recession some people may decide not to look for work. These people are called discouraged workers. They do not add to the unemployment rate because they are classified as not in the labor force rather than unemployed. Similarly, when the economy comes out a recession, more people may be encouraged to look for work. As they begin to look for jobs, they enter the labor force and add to the number of unemployed. Because of the phenomena of encouraged workers, the unemployment rate is sometimes slow to fall in the initial stages of recovery from a recession.

TYPES OF UNEMPLOYMENT AND THE NATURAL RATE OF UNEMPLOYMENT

There are many reasons a person might be unemployed. Economists group the reasons into three categories. One category is frictional unemployment. Frictional unemployment refers to people who are unemployed because they have just decided to enter the labor force, or they quit their old job to look for a better one, or they decided to move to a different place. A second category of unemployment is structural unemployment. Structural unemployment arises from significant changes in the economy. For instance, someone who worked as a typewriter repair person and loses her job because people switched from typewriters to computers is structurally unemployed. A textile worker who loses his job because merchants switched to imported textiles is also structurally unemployed. The last type of unemployment is called cyclical unemployment because it is associated with movements of the business cycle. During times when the economy is not producing up to its potential, resources are unemployed, including labor.

The different types of unemployment have very different consequences for the performance of the economy. Frictional and structural unemployment increase the efficiency of the economy in the long run. They are associated with people moving their labor from places where it is less valued to places where it is more valued. The rate of unemployment that exists when only frictional and structural unemployment exists is referred to by several different names: full employment rate of unemployment, the natural rate of unemployment, or the non-accelerating inflation rate of unemployment (NAIRU for short).

Cyclical unemployment is simply sacrificed output. If there is cyclical unemployment, we are giving up goods and services that labor could have produced. The existence of cyclical unemployment indicates that the economy is not operating as efficiently as it could be.

Unemployment is too high when it is higher than the natural rate. However, the natural rate of unemployment is not a constant. It changes over time, and it is very difficult to say what it is at any point in time. In the 1980s many economists thought the natural rate of unemployment was at least 6 percent, and that if the unemployment rate went much below 6 percent, then the rate of inflation would start to rise. In the 1990s the rate of unemployment fell below 5 percent, and not only did inflation not increase, it decreased.

MEASURING PRICES

The rate of inflation is the percentage change in the overall price level. There are several reasons to be concerned with inflation. If prices rise more rapidly than wages, then we are not able to buy as many goods and services as before. We have suffered a decline in real wages. Real wages are the actual amount of goods and services that we can buy with an hour's pay. Even if our money wages rise as rapidly as the price level and our real wages remain the same, we need to be concerned with inflation because when prices are all rising, markets do not work well. A business cannot tell whether the increase in price for its good is an increase in demand for it or just part of inflation. The business does not know whether it should increase or decrease production.

Measuring the change in the price level is much more difficult than measuring the change in the price of a single good. People buy thousands of goods each year. During a single year some prices go up, some go down, and some change very little.

Economists use the idea of a market basket to measure changes in the overall price level. Imagine that whenever you went to the supermarket, you picked up a basket and filled it with exactly the same things in the same quantities that you did last time. For instance, you buy one pound of hamburger, two apples, three oranges, a loaf of bread, and two boxes of macaroni and cheese. Although the prices of some goods may change more than others, you can tell how the price changes affect you by looking at the price of the basket as a whole.

The idea of a market basket is relatively straightforward. Goods such as a house or a car are actually baskets of goods that are sold together. A car is four wheels and tires, an engine, a transmission, seats, a steering wheel, and other components. People do not really care about the prices of the individual parts. It does not matter if the cost of the transmission is up if the price of the engine falls by more. We care about the price of the whole basket of things that make up a car. So we think of the basket of goods that make up a car as one good with one price.

Of course, not all the parts of the basket are of equal importance. A 5 percent increase in the cost of the transmission matters more to the overall price than a 5 percent increase in the price of the rearview mirror. Things that make up a larger part of the basket have greater weight in the final price. We do a similar thing to measure what is happening to the overall price level in the economy.

The market basket that receives the most attention is the basket that is used to calculate the Consumer Price Index (CPI). The CPI uses a basket that is meant to be representative of what a typical household in the United States consumes. As with the car, things that make up a larger part of household spending count for more than things that make up a small share. People consume both housing and pencils, but a 5 percent increase in the price of housing is much more important to them than a 5 percent increase in the price of pencils.

The CPI is one of many index numbers used in measuring economic performance. Business owners care about different prices than consumers

---

Calculating the CPI

The CPI for a particular year is the price of the market basket in that year divided by the price of the market basket in the base year, multiplied by 100. Mathematically it looks like the following:

CPI (2003) = (price of the basket in 2003 ÷ price of the basket in the base year) × 100.

Index numbers are by definition equal to 100 in the base year. If, on average, prices doubled since the base year, the market basket would cost twice as much and the CPI would be equal to 200.

do, so we use a different market basket to measure changes in the prices businesses pay for inputs. The Wholesale Price Index uses the market basket of goods that are typical for businesses to purchase. In addition, there are indices that describe things like industrial production. There are, of course, indices of stock market prices. In each case the objective is to describe the behavior of a group of things with a single number.

Measures of the price level have a number of uses. One of the uses is to adjust nominal values for changes in prices. For example, when examining the behavior of wages over time, it is useful to know what is happening to the real wage rather than the wage in current dollars. To change a nominal value into a real value, first divide the price index number (the CPI) by 100, then divide the nominal value by that number. Average hourly earnings in 2003 in current dollars were $15.35; the CPI was 184; and the base year was 1982. Dividing 184 by 100 gives us 1.84. Dividing $15.35 by 1.84 tells us that the real wage in 2003 was $8.34 in 1982 $s. This means that the $15.35 that the average worker received in 2003 purchased as much as $8.34 purchased in 1982.

Price index numbers are also used to convert a wage or a price into its equivalent for a different year. If you want to convert some price from year X into its equivalent for year Y, divide the price level in year Y by the price level in year X and multiply the result by the price in year X. For example, the average price of a barrel of crude oil in 1981 was $31. The average price in 2004 was $36. Which is more in real terms? We can find the 2004 equivalent for $31 in 1981 by dividing the 2004 CPI, which was 188.9, by the 1981 CPI, which was 90.9, to get 2.08. Prices on average were a little more than twice as high in 2004 as they had been in 1981. This is also the same as saying that dollars were about half as valuable in 2004 as they had been in 1981. Multiplying $31 by 2.08, we find that $31 in 1981 purchased as much as $64 did in 2004. The real cost of a barrel of oil was higher in 1981.

Table 2.4 shows the change in the CPI and some of its components from 1993 to 2004. Prices have not all changed by the same amounts or even in the same direction. Prices of clothing fell. Prices for medical care, on the other hand, increased about 50 percent. The difference between the index in any particular year and the base year is the percentage change since the base year. In 2002 the CPI was 179.9. The base year was 1983. So, according to the CPI, the cost of living had risen 79.9 percent since the base year. This 79.9 percent increase is not the rate of inflation.

The rate of inflation is the percentage change in the index from one year to the next, not the percentage change from the base year. For example, from 2002 to 2003 the CPI increased from 179.9 to 184, an increase of 4.1.

TABLE 2.4
CPI and Components, 1993–2004

Year	CPI	Food and beverages		Apparel	Housing	Transportation	Medical care	Education and communication
		Total	Food					
1993	144.5	141.6	140.9	133.7	141.2	130.4	201.4	85.5
2002	179.9	176.8	176.2	124.0	180.3	152.9	285.6	107.9
2003	184.0	180.5	180.0	120.9	184.8	157.6	297.1	109.8
2004	188.9	186.6	186.2	120.4	189.5	163.1	310.1	111.6

Source: Economic Report of the President, 2005. Table B-60, Consumer Price Indices for major expenditure classes.

The rate of inflation from 2002 to 2003 was 4.1 as a percentage of 179.9 (4.1 ÷ 179.9 = .022) or 2.2 percent.

Because it is possible to break the rate of inflation down into different components, such as housing, energy, and medical care, it is possible to estimate the core inflation rate. The core inflation rate removes the influence of changes in the prices of food and energy from the overall rate of inflation. The prices of food and energy tend to be more volatile than others; that is, they tend to go up and down more often and by larger amounts than most goods.

Using a fixed market basket of goods makes it easier to measure changes in the cost of living, but it also presents problems. The market basket attaches different importance, or weight, to different goods. A 5 percent increase in housing prices would have a larger impact on the CPI than a 5 percent increase in clothing prices, because housing is a larger share of our budget. The problem is that the goods that we consume do not stay fixed, and therefore the weight attached to different goods should not stay fixed. One reason our actual purchases do not stay fixed is that we try to minimize the impact of price increases on our budgets. As the price of a good increases, we switch to cheaper substitutes. New goods are introduced and we add them to our actual market baskets. The introduction of new goods is a big problem because the prices of new goods often fall in the first years after they are introduced into the market. For example, people bought VCRs for years before they were introduced into the CPI, and VCR prices fell dramatically during those years. Cellular telephones were not in the CPI until 1998, and the CPI did not include computers until 1990, when over 75 million Americans were already using them. The market basket used by the Bureau of Labor Statistics (BLS) is updated as well, but not as often as consumers change their consumption.

There is no general agreement about the effect of the difficulties in measuring changes in price. However, many economists believe that the CPI overstates increases in the cost of living by somewhere between 0.5 and 2 percent.

The degree to which inflation is overestimated is important because the government uses the CPI to adjust a number of government programs. For example, Social Security payments are adjusted for the effects of inflation to keep their real value from declining. Tax brackets are adjusted for inflation to keep people from being pushed into higher brackets by increases in the price level. Economists at the Brookings Institution concluded that eliminating the overestimation of inflation would reduce Social Security payments by $70 billion and increase tax revenue by $83 billion over the nine-year period from 2005 to 2014.

INTERNATIONAL COMPARISONS OF ECONOMIC PERFORMANCE

Within a single country we compare GDP in different years to talk about economic growth. We compare GDP between different countries to talk about relative levels of economic development. Both types of comparisons are complicated by the fact that prices of goods differ from year to year and country to country.

To see why changing prices is a problem, think about how we make international comparisons in GDP. To compare GDP per capita in different countries, we have to convert them to a single currency. Knowing that per capita GDP was $28,000 in the United States and 4,155,560 yen in Japan doesn't give us any information we can use. How do we convert yen into dollars so that we can compare the two? One way is to use the exchange rate: $1 = 120 yen. Table 2.5 shows comparisons of GDP in selected countries in 1996. Japanese per capita GDP seems to have been much higher than U.S. GDP per capita. But, actually, that was not the case. It only appeared that way because Japanese prices were much higher than U.S. prices. What can we do about this problem?

One approach to the problem of international comparisons is to use purchasing power parity (PPP) estimates. Purchasing power parity is the idea that a dollar (or peso, or whatever currency) should buy the same amount of goods in each country. We expect that, in the long run, exchange rates (prices of currencies; see chapter 8 for more details) will tend to adjust so that a dollar buys the same amount of goods and services in all countries. The reasoning is that if a dollar can buy more goods and services in Mexico than it can buy in the United States, then people will buy pesos and purchase Mexican goods. The increase in demand for pesos causes the value of the

Big Mac Purchasing Power Parity

The magazine *The Economist* developed a useful example of purchasing power parity using just the Big Mac. The cost of buying a Big Mac in 1997 in the United States was $2.43, while the cost in Israel was 13.9 shekels, which means that we would expect the exchange rate to be 5.27 shekels per dollar. This exchange rate would make the cost of the Big Mac equal in the two countries (at 5.27 shekels per dollar, $2.34 would buy you exactly 13.9 shekels, which you could use to buy a Big Mac in Israel). However, in 1997 the actual market exchange rate between Israeli shekels and U.S. dollars was 4.04 shekels per dollar.

peso to rise till a dollar buys the same amount in both countries. However, this does not happen completely. Some countries control their exchange rates rather than letting market forces determine them. In addition, not all goods flow freely across borders. Labor, especially, faces many restrictions. Purchasing power parity suggests what would happen to exchange rates without these complications.

To get around the problem that prices are not the same in all countries, we can calculate a PPP index that essentially tells us what the exchange rate would be if a dollar did buy the same amount of goods in every country. We can then use that hypothetical exchange rate to convert GDP of other countries into dollars.

Table 2.5 also shows per capita GDP in 1994 for several countries using World Bank PPP exchange rates. The figure for the United States stays the

TABLE 2.5
GNP Comparisons Using Actual Exchange Rates and PPP Exchange Rates, 1994

Country	GNP per capita ($s PPP method)	GNP per capita ($s official exchange rates)
United States	25,880	25,880
Japan	21,140	34,630
Russia	4,610	2,650
China	2,510	530
Haiti	930	230
Mozambique	860	90

Source: World Bank, *World Development Report, 1996.* New York: Oxford University Press, 1996.

same because U.S. prices are the standard that others are compared to in the estimation of the PPP index.

Avoiding being lied to with statistics is not easy. The government collects information and reports on a wide variety of measures of economic performance. People often select just the things that are most likely to support their views. Someone who wanted to paint a pessimistic picture of the economy in the 1970s and 1980s could show that real wages were lower in 1990 than in 1970. Someone who wanted to paint a more optimistic picture could show that real wages are only part of real compensation, which increased. But as we saw with the case of the CPI overestimating inflation, debates about measurement are not just semantic; billions of dollars are at stake.

Three

Economic Growth

The most distinctive feature of the American economy is the high rate of growth it has sustained over a long period of time. This chapter has three objectives: to show the benefits of long-run growth, to explain the causes of long-run growth, and to describe the long-run growth of the U.S. economy.

THE BENEFITS OF ECONOMIC GROWTH

Some people question the benefits of economic growth or argue that it cannot be sustained because of environmental constraints. There is, however, considerable evidence that economic growth does make people better off, does not necessarily damage the environment, and increases—not depletes—our stock of usable natural resources.

People are better off as a result of economic growth because they live longer, healthier lives, and they have more choices about how to live their lives. Some of the things we produce much more of now than we did in the past relate to health care and sanitation. Measles cases fell from over 500 cases for every 100,000 people in the United States in the 1930s to less than one case for every 100,000 people in the 1990s. Over the same period, tuberculosis cases fell from around 90 per 100,000 people to 7 per 100,000. Polio was eradicated from the developed world. In the 1930s, for each 10,000 births, 67 mothers died giving birth; by the 1990s less than one mother died for each 10,000 births. The average person born in 1900 could expect to live 47 years; the average person born in 1997 can expect to live until age 75.

TABLE 3.1
GNP and Life Expectancy, 1999

Income	GNP per Capita (1999 $s)	Life Expectancy at Birth (female)
Low Income	410	61
Middle Income	2,000	72
High Income	25,730	81

Source: The World Bank World Development Report, 2000–2001: Attacking Poverty. New York: Oxford University Press. Tables 1 and 2.

The effect of higher income on longevity is clear in international comparisons. Table 3.1 shows the relationship between GNP and life expectancy for low income, middle income and high income economies. In 1999, the average person in a high income country could expect to live two decades longer than the average person in a low income country.

Because of economic growth, we do not have to work nearly as long or as hard as people in the past. The average work week was 76 hours in 1830, 60 hours in 1890, 39 hours in 1950, and is just 34 hours today. In the nineteenth century, child labor was the norm in the United States, as it still is in many parts of the world. Children were sent to work because, by themselves, parents were not able to produce enough to feed, clothe, and shelter everyone in the family.

Because of economic growth, we get more goods and services even though we work less. In 1900, a Coke and a Hershey's bar each cost a nickel, but the average person had to work almost twenty minutes to earn that nickel. In 1997, a Coke cost 33 cents and a Hershey's bar cost 45 cents, but it took the average worker only 1.5 minutes to earn enough to buy the Coke and 2 minutes to buy the candy bar. For many other goods the changes have been even more dramatic. In 1908, it took the average person 4,696 hours to earn enough for a new car; in 1997, it took 1,365 hours. Moreover, the

---

Productivity Growth in Computing

The Productivity of a computer is measured in terms of millions of instructions carried out per second. In 1997 it was possible to purchase a computer that carried out 166 million instructions per second (MIPS) for $999. That price translates to $6 per MIPS. Each MIPS cost the average worker about 27 minutes' wages. In 1944, one MIPS cost the average worker 732,681 lifetimes worth of wages.

1997 model would have included an electronic ignition, air-conditioning, a stereo, and other amenities that were not available fifty years ago.

One common concern is that economic growth destroys the environment. The experience of America in the last fifty years does not bear this out. Even though we produce far more than we did thirty years ago, in many ways our environment is cleaner. Figure 3.1 shows that the annual emissions of several major air pollutants have decreased over the last thirty years, while the economy was growing. This is not to say that all pollution has been reduced, or that some types of production might not be harmful to the environment, but it does suggest that growth does not have to be associated with a decrease in the quality of the environment. As we become wealthier, one of the things we can choose to purchase is a cleaner environment.

Another concern is that economic growth cannot be sustained indefinitely because we will run out of natural resources. As one author put it, "We cannot long maintain our present rate of increase of consumption; . . . the cost of fuel must rise, perhaps within a lifetime, to a rate injurious to our commercial and manufacturing supremacy; and the conclusion is inevitable, that our present happy progressive condition is a thing of limited duration." Many people would agree with this author and say it is clear that eventually

FIGURE 3.1
Air Pollution Emissions in 1,000s of Tons, 1940–2000

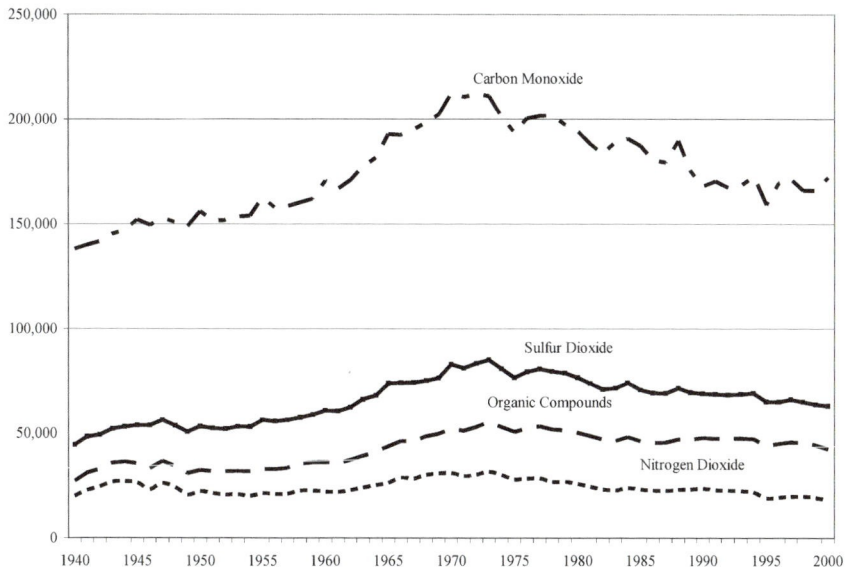

Source: Mini Historical Statistics, Hs-28. National Air Pollutant Emissions: 1900 to 2000, http://www.census.gov/statab/www/minihs.html

we will run out of oil. The author, however, is not describing current concerns about oil. The author was the English economist Stanley Jevons, writing in *The Coal Question* in 1865. England's happy progressive condition not only continued throughout the century after Jevons wrote, it continued at a more rapid pace than before. Jevons could not envision the extent to which new sources of energy would replace coal.

It is not blind optimism or faith in luck to believe that we will not run out of resources. Markets create incentives that prevent such a crisis. Crude oil itself provides an example of how market incentives prevent us from running out of resources. Most people are familiar with the story of *Moby Dick* by Herman Melville. In the story, Captain Ahab is obsessed with hunting down the great white whale, Moby Dick. But why were people from New England, like Ahab, sailing halfway around the world hunting gigantic aquatic mammals in the first place? It wasn't for sport and it wasn't because people then were unusually fond of whale meat. Whaling was a major industry in the United States because people needed whale oil to burn in lamps in order to have light in the evening. As people consumed more and more whale oil, whalers had to sail farther and farther to catch enough whales to satisfy demand. As the cost of whaling increased, the price of whale oil rose. The high price of whale oil set people searching for alternatives. One of these people was George Bissell. Bissell noticed that crude oil was flammable, and he wondered if it might be turned into a product that could substitute for expensive whale oil. He hired Benjamin Silliman, a chemist at Yale University, to explore the possibility of using crude oil to generate light. Crude oil was not considered an important resource until

---

Julian Simon's Wager

In 1980, economist Julian Simon challenged the environmentalist Paul Ehrlich to a bet. Ehrlich had been claiming that the earth was on course to run out of key resources in the next decade. If Ehrlich's prediction was correct, and key resources became very scarce, the prices of these resources would skyrocket over time. With this fact about markets in mind, Simon suggested they make a little wager. He offered to let Ehrlich pick a bundle of minerals worth $1,000 in 1980. If Ehrlich was right that the resources were being depleted, the bundle would cost more than $1,000 in 1990, and Simon would pay Ehrlich the difference. But if Ehrlich was wrong, the price of the bundle would not rise. If the bundle cost less than $1,000 in 1990, Ehrlich would pay Simon the difference. Ehrlich took the bet. By 1990, the price of the bundle had fallen to $618. The price of each of the goods Ehrlich had chosen was lower in 1990 than 1980.

Silliman discovered that it could be converted into kerosene. His discovery dramatically increased the amount of usable natural resources in the world.

Not only is economic growth associated with the discovery of new resources, but it encourages the more productive use of our existing resources. Kerosene lamps produced 20 percent more light than whale oil lamps. Edison's lightbulb produced sixteen times more light than the kerosene lamp, and fluorescent bulbs produce twenty-six times more light than Edison's bulb. A ton of coal produced 18 percent more kilowatt hours of electricity in 2002 than it did in 1950.

A LITTLE GROWTH GOES A LONG WAY

Economic growth brings Americans longer lives, more choices, and more resources. Remarkably, these advances have not even required a lot of growth each year. One of the most amazing things about long-run growth is how little is required each year in order for growth to make a big difference over a few decades. The wealthiest nations in the world have had long-term growth rates of per capita GDP of between 1 and 2 percent. The average growth rate of per capita GDP in the United States between 1820 and 1998 was 1.7 percent per year.

Using the Rule of 72, we can see the importance of small differences in the percentage rate of growth. The Rule of 72 states that if something grows at x percent per year, then it takes about $72 \div x$ years for the amount of the thing to double. If per capita GDP grows at 2 percent per year, it takes $(72 \div 2 =)$ 36 years for per capita GDP to double. If per capita GDP grows at 4 percent per year, then it takes only $(72 \div 4 =)$ 18 years for it to double.

When the growth rate is 1 percent, income slightly more than doubles in 100 years. When the growth rate is 2 percent, income rises to seven times its original level in 100 years. Creating a wealthy modern economy is about finding ways to get real per capita GDP to grow by around 2 percent per year, and then finding ways to sustain that growth.

THE CAUSES OF ECONOMIC GROWTH: INVESTMENT AND INNOVATION

Economic growth means producing more goods and services, and producing more goods and services is really not that mysterious a process.

Consider a simple example, the production of brownies. In order to produce brownies we need some ingredients: sugar, flour, baking soda, salt, butter, cocoa, eggs, and vanilla. We need tools: a cup and a spoon for measuring, a bowl and a spoon for mixing, and pans and an oven for baking. We need labor. Finally, we need a recipe. The recipe is crucial. We could not produce any brownies at all without the knowledge of how to combine the inputs in order to get the output.

There are really only two ways to increase brownie production. First, we can increase our inputs: more flour, more sugar, more pans, more time, and so on. Second, we can come up with a better way of doing things so that we can produce more brownies with the same amount of inputs.

This conclusion applies not just to brownies, but to all types of production. All types of production are alike in that they require inputs and they require knowledge about how to combine those inputs. It does not matter if we are talking about brownies or about GDP. If we want to increase production, we have to increase inputs or find ways to use the inputs we have more productively.

It would be possible to increase total output by adding more labor. Put more people in the workforce and make them all work harder. But most people would not think of that as real progress. What is generally desired is to increase output without having to do more work. In other words, the goal is to increase labor productivity. To increase labor productivity, we can use more of the other inputs, especially capital. Or we can introduce innovations that enable us to get more output from all of our inputs.

Saving and Investment

Saving and investment are crucial to economic growth. Giving workers more capital to work with, building more buildings and more machines, increases productivity. In addition, improvements in technology often require new factories and new equipment. For example, to take advantage of improvements in computer technology, we have to buy the new computer. Since investment is defined as the purchase of newly produced capital, we need to invest in order to accumulate more capital. To invest, we need to save. To save, we have to give up some current consumption. These relationships are true for personal finances, and they are equally true for the economy overall.

We have to consume less and save more in order to increase investment because we have limited resources. If we use resources to produce consumption goods, we can not use the same resources to produce capital goods. Think about GDP as a pie that is divided up between consumer goods, goods for the government, and capital goods. Suppose we have the resources and technology to produce $10 trillion worth of goods and services. If we decide to use part of our resources to produce $7 trillion in goods for consumers, and part of our resources to produce $1 trillion in goods for the government, then we have only enough resources left over to produce $2 trillion worth of capital goods. If we want more capital goods, we have to give up something else.

Financial Intermediaries and Investment

People do not usually transfer resources directly from consumption to investment. When people save, they put money into some financial intermediary. Financial intermediaries are firms like banks, credit unions, or some other firm that specializes in moving money from savers to borrowers. Businesses obtain funds from financial intermediaries in order to purchase new capital. When a person puts money in a bank he is really transferring control over part of society's resources. He is saying, "I have enough income to control $50,000 worth of society's resources, but I am not going to use all of it for consumption today. I am going to use only $40,000 of society's resources and let someone else decide how the other $10,000 should be used."

Financial intermediaries provide several benefits for savers. First, individual savers do not have to investigate all the possible business ventures themselves. Bank loan officers, mutual fund managers, and other financial intermediaries collect information from potential borrowers to determine where savings should go to. Second, financial intermediaries reduce risk for savers by enabling them to diversify their investments. Financial intermediaries are able to spread each individual's savings out among a large number of borrowers. In short, they enable people to follow the old rule of not putting all of their eggs in one basket.

Financial intermediaries play an important role in promoting growth. Without them it can be very difficult to get money from people who want to save to people who have good investment ideas. The more people save, the more financial intermediaries have available to lend. Increasing savings increases the supply of loanable funds and lowers the price of these funds, the interest rate. When interest rates fall, businesses borrow more and buy more new capital. More new capital means more growth.

USEFUL KNOWLEDGE AND INNOVATION

Although there are two ways to increase output, the two ways are not of equal importance in explaining long-run growth. Table 3.2 shows the relative importance of different factors in increasing production in the United States. Increases in inputs have played a smaller and smaller role over time,

TABLE 3.2
Percentage of Growth in Output Attributable to:

Years	Increase in Labor	Increase in Capital	Increase in Land	Increase in Productivity
1840–1860	49%	26%	10%	15%
1870–1930	43%	27%	4%	27%
1940–1990	41%	14%	0%	45%

Source: Jeremy Atack and Peter Passell, *A New Economic View of American History,* 2d ed., New York: Norton, 1994, p.19.

and productivity-enhancing innovations have now come to be the most important contributor to economic growth. Studies that compare different countries find similar results. Differences in productivity explain more than half of the differences in per capita income and growth between countries. Innovation, the introduction of better ways of doing things, is the most important source of economic growth, and it has become increasingly important over time.

Innovation that increases productivity requires both the development of useful knowledge and people who can put that knowledge to work in order to produce goods and services. "Useful" knowledge is knowledge about how the physical environment works that can be used to improve the production of goods and services. In the past, many societies developed extensive knowledge about religion, philosophy, and other disciplines, but not so much knowledge about how to produce things. In the last two hundred years, the United States and the other developed countries have developed a vast body of knowledge about how to produce goods and services.

Economic historian Joel Mokyr traces the growth of the last 200 to 300 years to the Scientific Revolution of the seventeenth century and the Industrial Enlightenment of the eighteenth century. The Scientific Revolution gave rise to our modern belief in the ability to understand the world through systematic research. The Industrial Enlightenment put systematic research to work at improving the production of goods and services. The Industrial Enlightenment was apparent in the spread of scientific societies, agricultural societies, societies of artisans and mechanics, journals, and encyclopedias. It created a culture in which useful knowledge grew like a snowball rolling downhill. People came to see the development of useful knowledge as one of the central functions of business, and research and development divisions became a standard component of large businesses.

The development of new ideas alone is not sufficient for innovation to have an impact on productivity in the economy. People have to implement the new ideas to produce goods and services. Recall that in the example of refining crude oil into kerosene, innovation took a chemist and an entrepreneur. Entrepreneurs are people who think they see better ways to use society's scarce resources. If they are right, then the resources are more valuable in their hands than in other people's hands. Henry Ford believed that labor was twice as valuable under his direction as it was under the direction of any other automobile manufacturer. He was right. Of course, entrepreneurs are not always right. John DeLorean also thought that the resources used to produce automobiles would be more valuable under his direction. Now the only time anyone sees the stainless steel DeLorean with its gull-winged doors is when they watch *Back To the Future*.

The market distinguishes between the entrepreneurs who are right and the ones who are not. Innovations that work are copied and expanded. Innovations that fail are eliminated from the market. Much like a process of natural selection, innovations that add value are able to gain a greater share of society's resources, while those that fail are unable to gain a claim on society's resources and die away.

Allowing people to fail is as important to growth in a market economy as allowing people to succeed. One economist who placed great emphasis on the benefits of failure was Joseph Schumpeter. Schumpeter argued that the most important incentive in market economies was the incentive to try to earn the high profits that come from doing something new—inventing a new good or service or a new way of producing a good or service. Schumpeter referred to innovation as "creative destruction" because at the same time it created new firms and new industries, it destroyed old ones. The creation of oil refining destroyed the whaling industry. The creation of the automobile destroyed the carriage industry. The creation of the personal computer destroyed the typewriter industry. Not all the firms in these industries were necessarily wiped out; some firms adapted to the changed circumstances. For example, the Fisher Carriage Company turned to the production of bodies for automobiles. But overall, the industries declined and resources flowed toward the production of the new and improved things.

INSTITUTIONS SHAPE INCENTIVES TO INVEST AND INNOVATE

Economic growth is the result of investment and innovation. Despite the simplicity of the recipe, most economic growth has occurred in only the last two hundred years, and many countries are still incredibly poor. To understand, why we have to return to the idea that all economic activity, including economic growth, is the result of people making choices.

TABLE 3.3
Time and Expense of Doing Business

Country	To Start a Small Business	To Resolve a Dispute in Court	Cost in weekly wages to fire a worker
United States	5 days	250 days	8 weeks
China	41	241	90
Czech Republic	40	300	22
Mexico	58	421	83
Brazil	152	566	165

Source: "In Brazil, Thicket of Red Tape Spoils Recipe for Growth," *Wall Street Journal*, Tuesday, May 24, 2005, A1.

Countries that have grown are countries where people have chosen to explore for new resources, to invest in new machines and equipment, and to develop new and better ways of doing things. People make these choices when they have the right incentives. They search for more useful knowledge when searching is encouraged. They save and invest when they are able to reap the rewards from their investments.

Throughout history, and in many parts of the world today, incentives do not encourage growth. In the former Union of Soviet Socialist Republics, many of the incentives discouraged productive behavior. Fame and fortune came through athletics or politics, not through coming up with a better car. In parts of Asia and Latin America, the returns from engaging in illegal drug production are several times the returns of producing food crops. In many parts of the world, incentives discourage people from starting businesses. Table 3.3 shows the time that it takes to accomplish various business activities in several countries. It is easy to see the difficulty a Brazilian entrepreneur faces relative to an American.

INSTITUTIONS ARE THE RULES OF THE GAME

The incentives in an economy are determined by its institutions. Douglass North, who won the 1993 Nobel Memorial Prize in economics for his work on institutions, describes institutions as "the rules of the game." The comparison with games is particularly appropriate because it illustrates the influence of incentives on behavior. It is not unusual to see baseball players bumping up against the official as they argue a call. You seldom see such behavior in a football game. The difference is not because football players are naturally more gentle and civil than baseball players. The difference is

Innovation "drives" economic growth; the transition from horse-drawn carriage to automobile is one of the classic examples. Getty Images: The Palma Collection.

because the penalties for such behavior are much greater in football. Professional sports leagues are strong believers in the effectiveness of incentives. If the NBA wants a faster basketball game, it creates a 24-second rule. If the NHL wants more scoring, it decreases the size of goalie pads.

In economies, the rules of the game—the institutions—are comprised of the formal laws that have been enacted and informal rules of behavior. The most important types of rules for encouraging economic growth are rules that protect property rights, rules that make it easier to trade, and rules that encourage people to continually create and share new knowledge.

Formal Rules

Institutions that protect property rights ensure that the person who is choosing how to use a valuable resource is the person who receives the benefits or pays the costs of that choice. When property rights are clear and well enforced, people have the right to buy and sell their property. They have the right to use their property as they see fit as long as it does not harm others. And they have the right to receive the income from using their property. Thus, when property rights are clear and well enforced, people have an incentive to make sure that the resources they own are used where they are most valued. They also have an incentive to protect their resources and make sure that their resources are not damaged or wasted.

Institutions that make trading easier help people engage in trades that make them better off. Many trades are uncomplicated. When a person goes into Starbucks to buy three pounds of Italian-roast coffee beans in exchange for thirty dollars, both the buyer and seller know exactly what they are getting, and the exchange is simultaneous. Not all trades are so simple. When a trade is complicated, a person may have to take steps to make sure that the trade is truly mutually beneficial. When a person buys a house, for instance, she may hire a real estate agent to help her look; when she finds a place, she hires an inspector to look for defects in the house; she hires an exterminator to check for termites; she pays for a title search to make sure that the person she plans to buy the house from has the legal right to sell it. All of these things create a gap between the total cost of the house to her and the price that the seller receives. Exchanges that take place over time rather than simultaneously are also complicated. When a bank lends money to someone, how can they ensure that it will be repaid? They may screen their customers beforehand. They may require a contract that provides collateral, such as a house. These things also create a gap between what a buyer pays and what a seller receives. The costs that make up these gaps are called transaction costs.

Transaction costs are low when an exchange is uncomplicated. Transaction costs are high when the good is complicated or when the trade takes place over time. Legal institutions like contract law help lower transaction costs by raising the cost of not fulfilling a contract.

Informal Rules

Although formal rules, such as laws, are important, informal rules may be even more important. Informal rules are social norms of behavior that are not enforced by the government but are enforced by society. Without informal rules that encourage honest behavior, laws mean little. Contract law is useful only if you believe that the judge will decide your case impartially.

Once when I was grading an exam on law and the economy, a student referred to an old expression, "He who does not steal steals from his family." You may not have heard this old expression before. I had not. But it was clear that the student believed that it was common knowledge. He was from an Eastern European country where communism had just recently ended. The meaning of the expression is that corruption is not only acceptable, it is the moral thing to do: If we do not take bribes, we are harming the people who depend on us most, our family. Once such a view becomes widely held, it is difficult to support a market economy, and such informal institutions can be very difficult to change.

What Determines the Rules of the Game?

Economic institutions are the rules of the game, but they are determined by politics and culture, and those games are played by their own rules. Exactly what political rules give rise to good economic institutions is a subject of intense research by social scientists today. Some believe that democracy promotes economic growth by preventing despots from infringing on individual freedoms. Others believe that democracy can hamper economic growth by allowing interest groups like unions or trade associations to gain special interest legislation, such as protective tariffs. Research on the relationship between political, social, and economic institutions has not yet reached the point where it is possible to present any definitive conclusions. Research on the evolution of informal institutions is even more in its infancy than research on the evolution of formal institutions. What we can do here is examine the economic development of the United States and consider how its institutions evolved to encourage investment and innovation.

THE GROWTH OF THE AMERICAN ECONOMY

THE COLONIAL FOUNDATIONS

The origins of the United States of America can be traced to an attempt to make a profit. The first permanent English colony was the Jamestown colony in Virginia. Jamestown was the venture of a corporation named the London Company. The first settlers hoped to discover riches and make a quick buck. They found that there was no gold or silver and that making a living in Virginia would require some effort; most of the first settlers died. After some experimentation, the settlers discovered goods, most notably tobacco, that could be profitably grown and exported to England.

Colonists in other parts of the country made money from products and services that exploited the natural resources at their disposal. Southerners raised tobacco (America's largest single export during the colonial era), rice, indigo, and a little cotton. Settlers in the mid-Atlantic region specialized in grain production and trade. New Englanders focused on trade, shipping, timber and other products from their forests, and fishing.

Before the American Revolution, most of the people who came from the Old World to the New World were indentured servants. Many people in England found the prospect of moving to the New World to seek their fortunes an attractive one, but the cost of getting there was more than a year's wages for the average worker in England. Indentured servants contracted to work in the colonies for a period of time, for instance seven years; the buyer of the indenture contract paid the cost of their trip to the New World.

The colonies encouraged immigration. Often a colonist could receive a grant of land from a colony by paying his own way over, and a colonist could receive additional land for each additional person that he brought over. Rapid immigration combined with a high birth rate led to a rapidly growing population. By 1776 the population of the thirteen original colonies had reached around 2 million. Income and life expectancy were comparable to those in England.

The colonists brought with them the basic legal system of England, the common law. Common law was not created by legislators; it had evolved over time as judges decided individual cases. Recent studies have found that countries with a common law tradition have higher rates of growth than those without common law. A common law tradition is associated with greater protection of property rights and greater financial market development because the common law evolved in England to protect individual property rights. In contrast, French civil law developed to solidify state control and reign in judges.

British colonists also brought with them the ideas of the Scientific Revolution and the Industrial Enlightenment. Ben Franklin, Thomas Jefferson, and George Washington were not only political leaders, but inventors, entrepreneurs, and investors. All three were influenced by the belief that systematic study could lead to useful knowledge and better ways of making things. Washington and Jefferson experimented with different methods of producing and harvesting crops. Washington supported agricultural societies to spread new knowledge about production. Franklin went furthest as a scientist, inventor, entrepreneur, and advocate for the extension of useful knowledge. He is widely known for his studies of electricity and his inventions of the lightning rod, bifocals, and the Franklin stove. In 1748 he proposed establishing the American Philosophical Society for "Promoting Useful Knowledge Among the British Plantations in America." He also built his own successful business in publishing.

None of the founding fathers invented any product or business that significantly shaped American economic growth. Jefferson, for instance, was not even particularly adept at business; at the time of his death he was in considerable debt. What is noteworthy is that America's political elite tied themselves so strongly to a belief in the promotion of useful knowledge and entrepreneurship. The United States is a nation founded by entrepreneurs. Its statesmen were also businessmen.

Many of the issues that led to the American Revolution were directly related to the economy, but for most of the revolutionaries it would have been difficult to separate what was economic and what was political. For many of them a large part of liberty was liberty to produce, to buy, and to sell without government interference. In addition to "taxation without representation," the English government interfered in foreign trade between the colonies and other countries, limited westward expansion, and granted a monopoly of the trade in tea to one company. Farmers who sought to export their crops, entrepreneurs who invested in unsettled lands in the West, and merchants all had reasons to believe the British government was impinging on their liberty and their economic success.

THE CONSTITUTION AND EARLY AMERICAN DEVELOPMENT

During the Revolution and up until 1789, the federal government operated under the Articles of Confederation. The Articles of Confederation granted very little power to the federal government. The federal government had to ask states for contributions because it had no power to tax. The federal government had no control of money. States could create barriers to trade not only with foreigners but with people in other states. Each state was law unto itself.

The Constitution was the result of an effort to strengthen the federal government, and at the same time to ensure that the federal government did not become a threat to liberty. People often emphasize the democratic nature of American government, but early Americans were as concerned with liberty as with democracy. James Madison thought that the fundamental problem of government was how to have a democracy and at the same time protect individual rights so that a majority could not deprive a minority of its rights. Given their concern with economic liberty, it should not be surprising that when the former revolutionaries got together to draft a Constitution, they sought to protect property rights and encourage free markets. The Constitution prohibits states from creating barriers to trade with people in other states or nations.

The Constitution ensured that, at least in terms of the law, the United States would be one market. It created what Europeans are still struggling to create through the European Common Market, a single market over most of a continent. The part of the Constitution that gives the federal government authority over trade between the states is called the "commerce clause." The commerce clause is the Constitutional foundation for most federal regulation.

The Constitution prohibits states from passing laws that impair the obligation of contracts in the "contract clause." The Constitution empowers the federal government to coin money and to create uniform laws for intellectual property rights, immigration, and bankruptcy. The Constitution also put in place certain restrictions to protect liberty. The Fifth Amendment prohibits the taking of life, liberty, or property without due process, and it requires that just compensation be paid when the government does take someone's property.

In addition to the specific rules intended to restrict political power, the rules for the political system are designed to spread power across the branches of government and prevent legislators from passing laws that diminish liberty. Within the federal government, a system of checks and balances protects minorities from majorities. In addition, although the Constitution provides the federal government with much power, states retain much of their power to tax, to spend, and to pass their own laws.

The federal system, a system of independent state governments and an overarching federal government established by the Constitution, supports economic growth in two ways. First, states compete with each other to attract people and businesses. If one state raises taxes too high or passes laws that discourage business, people go to another state. Second, having multiple state governments allows for experimentation. States experiment with different types of banking legislation, different rules for corporations, and different degrees of support for public transportation and education. Experiments that are successful in one state tend to be copied in other states.

The federal system also made it relatively easy for different states to develop along different paths. The North led the way in developments in finance, transportation, education, and manufacture. By 1850, manufacturing output per person had reached $104 in New England and $74 in the mid-Atlantic. In contrast, it was $21 per person in the Midwest and only $12 per person in the South. By 1860 there was more than $22 of bank money per person in the North and mid-Atlantic as opposed to $11 in the South Atlantic and $13 in the Southwest.

Cotton and Slavery in the South

A single innovation played a major role in shaping the development of the South. In 1793, a young man from New England who had come to the South as a teacher invented a cotton gin. Eli Whitney's cotton gin removed seeds from short staple cotton. Short staple cotton is the variety of cotton that grows best in the United States, but it contains many small seeds that are difficult to remove by hand. The first cotton gin was little more than a box with a wire screen and wire hooks on the inside and a crank on the outside, but it enabled one person to do in hours what before it had taken many people days to do. The device was brilliant in its simplicity. (It was, in fact, so simple that it was virtually impossible for Whitney to exercise his patent rights. People all over the South made their own gins.)

After the invention of the cotton gin, cotton became king in the South. In 1794 the United States exported 1.6 million pounds of cotton; six years later it exported 18 million pounds of cotton. In the 1850s cotton exports averaged over 1 billion pounds per year. In 1860, total exports of merchandise were valued at $316 million, of which $192 million was cotton.

With cotton came slavery. Why cotton, slavery, and the South are intertwined is a subject that has long been debated. Most economic historians now believe that it is mostly the result of the available technologies for producing cotton. Cotton required large amounts of intensive and difficult labor at specific times during the year. At the time, the cheapest way to grow a lot of cotton was to use what is called a "gang labor system." The gang system relied on specialization and division of labor. Slaves worked as a group, or gang. In planting, one group of slaves would move in first, opening small holes; the next group would follow, dropping seeds into the holes; and the third group would follow, raking dirt over the holes. All would of course be driven as fast as they could. The largest plantations were able to obtain the greatest specialization and division of labor and the greatest output. Farmers with over 100 acres held 90 percent of all slaves and produced 86 percent of all cotton.

Manufacturing in the North

Cotton also played a prominent role in Northern development. Although it is not possible to cultivate cotton in the North, the North developed a cotton textile industry.

England was the dominant cotton textile producer in the 1700s, and England prohibited the transfer of its technology to other countries. While the law was able to keep people from shipping textile equipment or plans, it was not able to keep people from bringing the knowledge that was in their heads. Samuel Slater used the knowledge that he gained working in British textile mills to help start the first American textile mill in 1790. Francis Cabot Lowell used the knowledge that he gained from a tour of an English factory to start the Boston Manufacturing Company and build the first integrated mill—a mill for both spinning thread and weaving cloth—in the United States in 1831. As the size of its factories increased, the Boston Manufacturing Company, recruited young women from rural areas and built dormitories in which to house them, a practice that many Chinese factory managers still copy today.

Soon the American industrial revolution spread to other types of manufacture and took on a distinctively American style. By the middle of the nineteenth century Europeans were talking about an American System of manufacture. The American System was characterized by the production of simple, sturdy goods composed of interchangeable parts. In the past, things like firearms had been manufactured by hand by craftsmen. No two were exactly alike. Each part was specifically crafted to fit with the other parts. American manufactures innovated the use of interchangeable parts to create cheap but useful goods. The movement began in firearms with Eli Whitney and Samuel Colt, then with Singer in sewing machines and McCormick in reapers. Completely interchangeable parts were not achieved until the 1870s when metalworking and machine tools became more precise, but the idea was one that would play a prominent role in American industrialization.

State and local governments supported the growth of the economy by supporting improvements in transportation. Many communities provided funds for roads, and state and local governments provided support for canals, and later railroads. The most notable state investment was the Erie Canal. The Erie Canal was notable not only for its size, but because it was one of the few transportation projects that was financially successful.

States also promoted economic growth through development of financial markets by allowing private commercial banks to operate. There were no commercial banks prior to the Revolution. By 1815, states had chartered over two hundred banks. By 1860 there were 1,562 state banks with $254 million in deposits.

The banks and the railroads were made possible by states' grants of corporate charters. The advantage of the corporate form to investors is that corporations usually have limited liability; that is, the liability of investors is limited to the money spent to buy the stock. Limited liability made it possible to raise large amounts of money to finance big businesses (see chapter 5). Because people knew they could not lose more than they had put into the corporation, they were willing to invest even if they did not have a large enough number of shares to influence how the company was run.

A corporate charter was not easily obtained before the nineteenth century. The legislature passed a special law to create each chartered corporation. Eventually, states came to adopt general charter rules. Today, if an entrepreneur wants to form a corporation, he needs only to fill out the right forms and agree to abide by the rules established by the state.

New Technologies and the Rise of Big Business

In 1860 the United States was still dominated by agriculture and small-scale production, but the seeds had been sown for the next stage of economic development. The Constitution made the United States a single market in law. Canals, railroads, and telegraphs supplemented the natural system of transportation provided by America's lakes, rivers, and ocean ports, making a single market a reality. States had created rules for granting corporate charters, which made it possible to raise large amounts of investment funds. When people developed new technologies of mass production in the late nineteenth century, the United States was uniquely positioned to take advantage of them.

Mass production relies on economies of scale for its profitability. Economies of scale occur when it is cheaper to produce goods in large quantities than in small quantities. The automobile assembly line provides a good example. An assembly line requires large investments in factory and equipment, but it is a very efficient way of producing thousands of cars. On the other hand, the assembly line is not a very cost-effective way of producing twelve cars. In the late nineteenth century, several new methods of mass production were developed in major industries. The companies that were able to exploit these new technologies came to dominate their industries: John D. Rockefeller's Standard Oil Company, Andrew Carnegie's Carnegie Steel Works, August Busch's Anheuser Brewing, James Buchanan Duke's American Tobacco Company.

The United States also benefited from a bit of good fortune during this period. Many of these new technologies required a lot of natural resources. For example, while it required a lot of new technology and a lot of capital to build a car, it also required a lot of steel to make the car and a lot of oil to make it go. The United States not only had natural resources, but it had them in places that were relatively easy to access.

The late nineteenth and early twentieth century was a period of rapid growth, driven by a combination of resource abundance, rapid capital accumulation, and technological development. The peak of this rapid growth came during the 1920s. From the standpoint of economic history, the Roaring Twenties are aptly named. The twenties had the highest rate of productivity growth in American history. From 1917 to 1927, productivity growth averaged 3.8 percent per year. This productivity growth was reflected in major changes in the way people lived.

The Roaring Twenties and Great Depression

One thing that deserves much of the credit for the Roaring Twenties is the extension of electricity to both businesses and homes. Electricity is an example of a general purpose technology. General purpose technologies are ideas that can be applied to many different activities, like the internal combustion engine, microchips, and electricity. For businesses, electricity made possible revolutionary improvements in production. No longer did a factory have to be designed around its power source. Now energy could be brought wherever it was needed by a couple of wires; each piece of equipment could have its own electric motor. When the motor broke down on one piece of equipment, it did not affect the power in the rest of the factory. For households, the changes were equally dramatic. People could have electric light to read by in the evening; they could keep food fresh in an electric refrigerator; they could get news and entertainment from a radio.

The Roaring Twenties came to a crashing halt late in 1929. Real output fell from 1929 to the early part of 1933. Unemployment rose to 25 percent of the labor force. Banks failed by the thousands. The Great Depression was neither the first nor the last recession in the United States, but it was the most severe (see chapter 4). Not until 1940 did the United States regain the level of production that it had in 1929. Although some people at the time thought that economic growth had come to an end with the Great Depression, it turned out to be a temporary setback, although a long and unpleasant one.

The Postwar Economy

During World War II, output soared and unemployment fell to abnormally low levels. The two decades after the Second World War witnessed growth rates of productivity that came close to the growth of the 1920s. From 1950 to 1973, increases in output per hour of labor averaged 2.7 percent per year. At the same time, both unemployment and inflation remained relatively low.

In the 1970s and 1980s, productivity growth slowed. From 1973 to 1985, productivity growth averaged only 1.5 percent per year. Remember how important small differences in growth rates are. Something growing at 2.7 percent a year doubles every 26 years. Something growing at 1.5 percent a year takes 48 years to double.

Among economists there are two approaches to explaining the low productivity growth of the 1970s and 1980s. One approach is to explain the low productivity growth rates as the result of changes in labor markets, the oil market crises of the 1970s, increased government regulation, and a decline in innovation. The second approach is to argue that although there may have been some slowdown in productivity growth, it has probably been exaggerated. Economists who take the second approach believe there are many errors in the measurement of productivity.

Arguments for an actual slowdown in productivity growth rates include the following. First, because baby boomers and more women came into the labor force, the number of inexperienced workers increased during the 1970s. Workers with less job experience tend to be less productive. Second, there were large unanticipated increases in the price of energy, and energy costs accounted for about 14 percent of GDP in the mid-1970s. The cost of producing nearly everything went up, so supply went down. Third, there was a significant increase in federal regulation in the 1960s and 1970s. The federal government established the Environmental Protection Agency, the Consumer Product Safety Commission, and the Occupational Safety and Health Administration. Businesses had to use resources to meet the new regulations that these agencies established. Fourth, businesses invested a lot of money in the development of new information technology, but computers did not yet have much of an impact on productivity.

While there is a strong argument for a slowdown in productivity growth, it is also clear that we have done a poor job of measuring productivity. It is not because we haven't tried to measure productivity; considerable effort has been made for decades. But measuring productivity is difficult, and productivity has become increasingly difficult to measure over time. The reason that it has become so much more difficult to measure productivity today is because of the rapid introduction of new products and improvements in the quality of products. It is much easier to count changes in the output of steel and wheat than changes in the output of medical care or information processing. A desktop computer built in 1990 and one built in 2000 may

FIGURE 3.2
Changing Distribution of the Workforce, 1840–2000

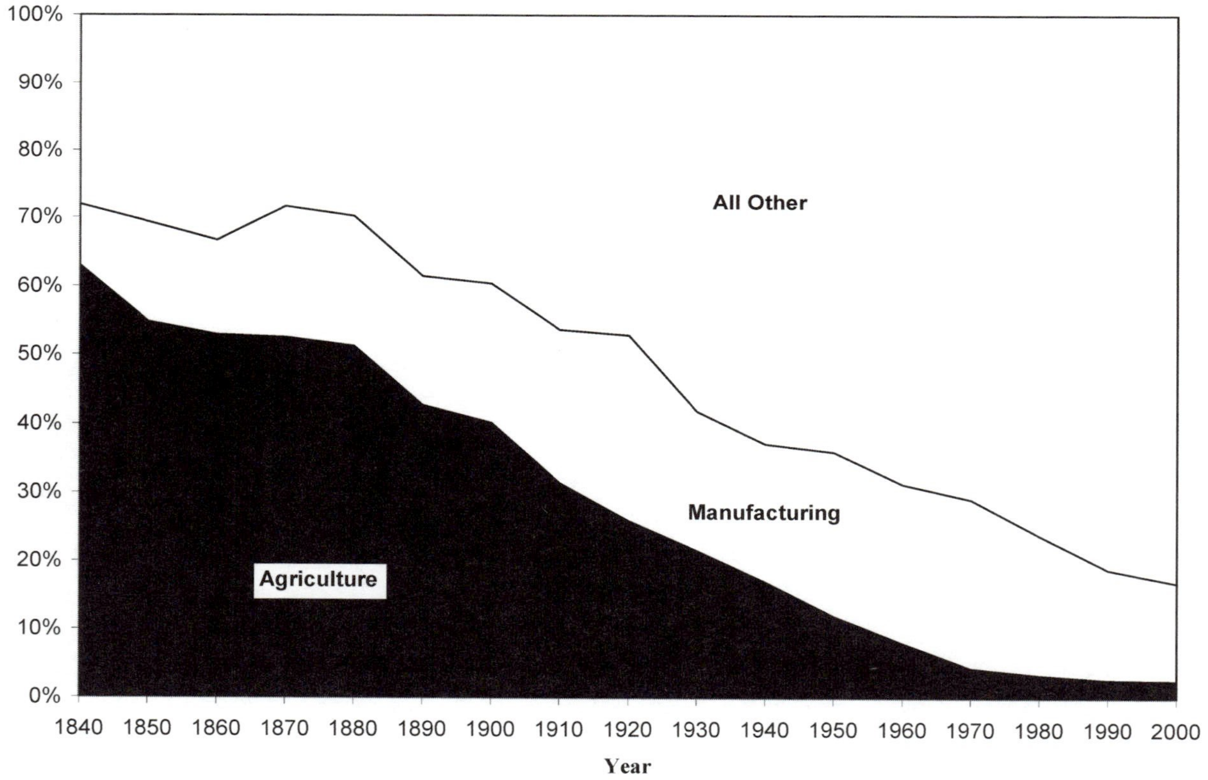

Source: U.S. Census Bureau, *Historical Statistics of the United States on CD-ROM, Colonial Times To 1970 Bicentennial Edition*, Series D 167–181, Labor Force and Employment, by Industry; and Mini Historical Statistics, No. HS-29, Employment Status of the Civilian Population: 1929 to 2002, http://www.census.gov/statab/www/minihs.html

look similar, but—as anyone who bought both knows—they are not. The newer computer had much more for a much lower price.

Although the rate at which productivity was growing may have slowed in the 1970s and 1980s, it did continue to grow. In the two hundred years from 1789 to 1989, investment and innovation completely transformed the American economy. The transformation in the structure of the economy during nineteenth and twentieth centuries can be seen in Figure 3.2, which shows the distribution of the labor force from 1840 to 2000. The percentage of the labor force in agriculture has continued to shrink throughout American history. By 1840 it had already fallen from the 90 percent of the workforce that it had been in the seventeenth and eighteenth centuries to below 70 percent. By the end of the twentieth century the percentage of the labor force in agriculture had fallen below 3 percent.

THE NEW ECONOMY

Structural changes in the economy in the last decade of the twentieth century were sufficiently noticeable that many people began to talk about a "new economy." The primary characteristic of the new economy was an increase in the rate of productivity growth. Because of the difficulty of measuring productivity growth, there was at first considerable debate about whether a significant increase in the rate of productivity growth was actually taking place. But by the early 2000s, it was clear that the productivity slowdown of the 1970s and 1980s had ended. From 1995 to 2003, productivity growth averaged 3.2 percent.

By the 1990s many of the factors that were suggested as causes of the productivity slowdown had been reversed. The labor force was more mature. Energy prices had fallen, and energy costs accounted for a smaller portion of GDP. Beginning with the Carter administration in the late 1970s, attempts were made to roll back regulation in industries such as transportation, communication, and finance. Developments in information technology were finally paying off with innovations that improved productivity, and businesses invested in new plant and equipment to take advantage of these innovations.

Observation of everyday life appears to support the productivity data and suggests that the rate of innovation accelerated during the 1990s and the first decade of the twenty-first century. In 1985, most college students, like students for decades before them, went to the library to do research with books and journals, took handwritten notes, and typed papers on typewriters while listening to vinyl records. In 2005, students use laptop computers, smaller than portable typewriters, to access more research material online than was available in many college libraries in the 1980s. They type up

FIGURE 3.3
Average Annual Increases in Productivity, 1873–2003

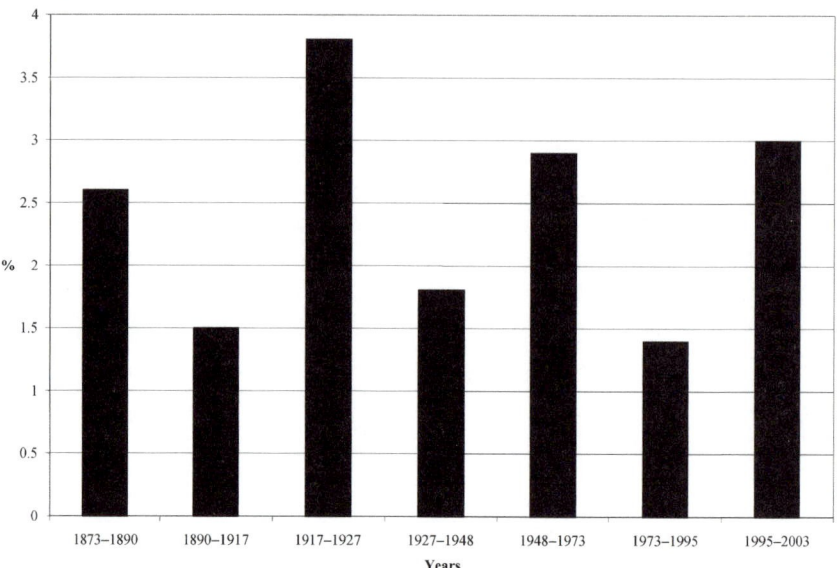

Source: Roger W. Ferguson and William Wascher, "Distinguished Lecture on Economics in Government: Lessons from Past Productivity Booms," *Journal of Economic Perspectives* 18 (2004): 3–28.

papers on the same laptop using a word processing program that points out spelling and grammatical errors, and allows them to edit by cutting and pasting without having to retype anything. The vinyl records, first replaced by CDs, are now replaced by other electronic forms of music storage, with thousands of songs stored in devices the size of an old tape cassette. They carry phones smaller than a wallet, and the phones can make calls, store phone numbers, send text messages, receive voice mail, take and send video images, store information, and serve as a calculator.

Although there is evidence that we are in the middle of a "new economy," it should be kept in mind that it is not the first "new economy." Figure 3.3 shows how the rate of productivity growth has risen and fallen repeatedly since the 1880s. The essence of economic growth is to create new economies all the time. Sometimes the rate of productivity growth is more rapid than at others times, but as long as the United States continues to provide institutions that encourage investment and innovation, it is reasonable to expect that productivity will continue to grow.

Four

Business Cycles

On October 28, 1929, the value of the stocks listed on the New York Stock Exchange fell $18 billion. GDP fell from late 1929 until early 1933. In real terms, output was 29 percent lower in 1933 than it had been four years earlier; prices were 24 percent lower. The number of commercial banks declined by ten thousand between 1929 and 1933, and the money supply (M1) fell by over $5 billion. The unemployment rate reached 25 percent in 1933. Output increased again from 1933 until 1937, but unemployment remained over 10 percent; it was not until 1939 that GDP was as high as it had been in 1929. Because of the severity of the decline and the slow recovery, the 1930s became known as the Great Depression.

About ten years before the Great Depression began in the United States, Germany experienced a different economic problem—not falling prices, but rising prices. At one point prices rose 43 percent each day. As I am writing this, on the first day of July 2005, a gallon of gas costs about $2.20, up considerably from last year. If prices were to rise at 43 percent per day, by the end of the month a gallon of gas would cost $63,940. That's not a typo. To fill up a fifteen-gallon tank at the end of the month would cost almost $1 million.

Because of the rapid rate of inflation, German factory workers were paid each day. Foremen threw bundles of German marks to the workers, who ran out to buy anything they could get their hands on, just to get rid of the money before its value declined further. Prices rose in a German café between the time a customer sat down and the time she left. The German printing presses could not keep up. Eventually the German government was printing 1 trillion mark notes. One U.S. dollar bought over 4 trillion marks. Many Germans found the value of their life's savings wiped out in a matter of months. The money they had accumulated over years of work no longer bought even a cup of coffee.

BUSINESS CYCLES

These two stories illustrate the problems of economic instability, the short-run ups and downs called business cycles. The first is an extreme example of a recession. A business cycle begins with an expansion, during which real GDP is increasing. The end of the expansion is called the peak of a business cycle. The peak is followed by a contraction during which real GDP is decreasing. Periods of decreasing real GDP are called recessions. Technically, an economy is declared to be in recession when real GDP declines for six months. The lowest point of a contraction is called the trough of the business cycle. The official dating of business cycles is done by a private nonprofit research organization, the National Bureau of Economic Research. Between 1945 and 1991 the United States experienced eight business cycles. Contractions lasted an average of 10 months and expansions lasted an average of 52 months. The United States then experienced a remarkable 120-month expansion from March 1991 to March 2001, followed by a brief recession before growth resumed.

The Great Depression more than qualifies as a recession since output fell for nearly three years. The Great Depression also differs from most recessions because even after output started to increase again, it did so very slowly.

Post–World War I Germany illustrates an extreme version of inflation called hyperinflation. Like the Great Depression, the German hyperinflation was an almost complete breakdown of the economy. Markets could no longer function because prices lost all meaning as indicators of supply and demand.

Although the primary determinant of the standard of living is the long-run rate of growth, people are often more concerned with economic instability. When you cannot find work, or when you see the value of your savings being destroyed by inflation, it is hard to focus on the long run. Figures 4.1 and 4.2 show how the rate of inflation and the unemployment rate have fluctuated over time in the United States. Short-run fluctuations in the economy have often led to demands that something be done about the economy. During President Clinton's first campaign, his adviser James Carville posted signs that said, "It's the economy, Stupid." The signs were intended to remind everyone that the focus of Clinton's campaign should be the recession in 1991, and the promise that they could do a better job on the economy.

In order to evaluate the demands for government action and politicians' promises to respond, it is necessary to know something about what causes

FIGURE 4.1
Rate of Inflation, 1914–2002

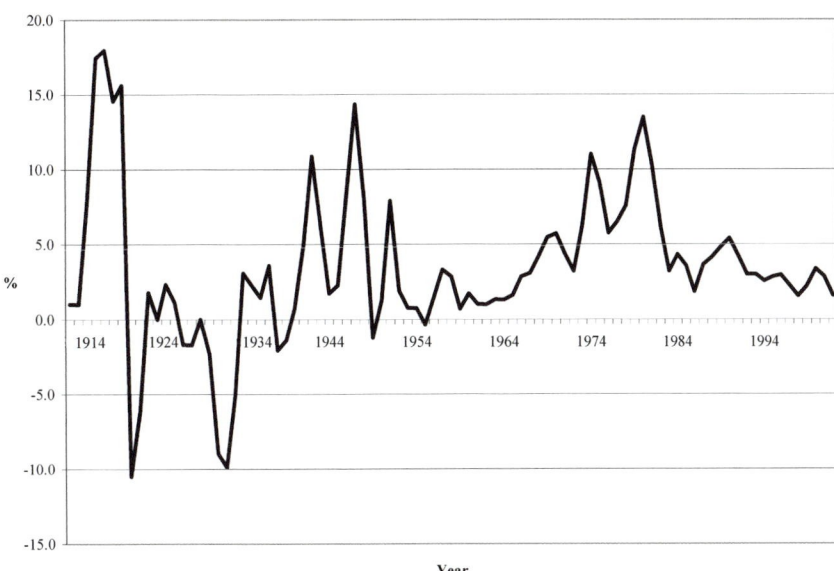

Source: Mini Historical Statistics, No. HS-36, Consumer and Gross Domestic Price Indexes: 1913 to 2002, http://www.census.gov/statab/www/minihs.html

FIGURE 4.2
Unemployment Rate, 1929–2002

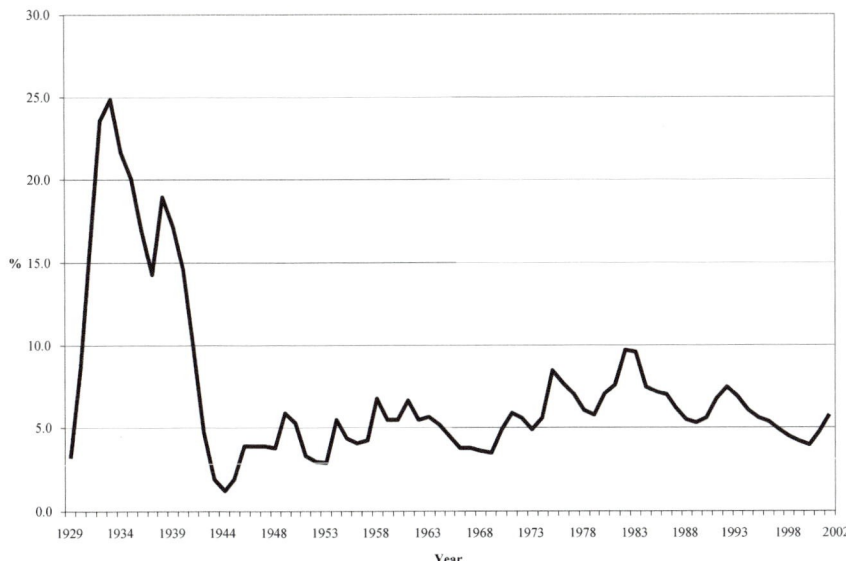

Source: Mini Historical Statistics, No. HS-29, Employment Status of the Civilian Population: 1929 to 2002, http://www.census.gov/statab/www/minihs.html

the economy to depart from its potential output and what tends to drive it back to that potential.

POTENTIAL OUTPUT

In both the cases of recession and inflation, the problem is that the economy departs from its potential output. Potential output is the level of output that is produced when the economy is at its natural rate of unemployment. The natural rate of unemployment is the one that exists when there is only frictional and structural unemployment.

It is possible for output to fall below its potential. Such was the case during the Great Depression. In the short run, it is also possible to push the economy past its potential output. For instance, during major wars, economies are often pushed past their potential. People who might not have entered the labor force under normal circumstances enter during the war. Other people work more than they ordinarily would. During such periods, prices rise rapidly. In the United States, periods of war have always been associated with inflation.

The fact that prices rise when output is pushed past its potential leads to another way of characterizing potential output. Potential output can be thought of as the most goods and services the economy can produce without inflation increasing. Because of this relationship between output, unemployment, and inflation, some people call the natural rate of unemployment the NAIRU (Non-Accelerating Inflation Rate of Unemployment). The NAIRU concept emphasizes the idea that if we keep trying to increase output and reduce unemployment below this level, the ultimate result is accelerating inflation. Accelerating inflation means that prices are not only increasing, but that they are increasing at a quicker and quicker rate.

Why would a country produce less than it did the year before? There are really just two possibilities. The first possibility is that the country is simply not able to produce as much as the year before. The potential output has fallen. This was the explanation for decreases in output for most of human history. Output fell because a drought or a flood destroyed the crops. Output fell because war or disease killed people. In many countries, war and natural disasters are still important factors influencing short-run changes in GDP.

A decrease in our ability to produce goods and services does not, however, provide a very good explanation for the Great Depression or most of the other recessions the United States has experienced. We were capable of producing at least as much in 1930 as 1929, yet we did not. The labor, the factories, and the farms were still there. All the knowledge for how to produce goods and services was still there. Yes, there was the Dust Bowl; the 1930s was definitely a bad decade for agriculture in some parts of the country, but the problems in agriculture are not enough to explain the catastrophic decline in output in a country that was no longer predominantly agricultural.

Since a decrease in our ability to produce goods and services does not seem to provide an adequate explanation for recessions, we turn to the second possibility. The second possibility is that, for some reason, firms choose not to produce as much as they are capable of producing. This possibility is the more puzzling of the two. Why would people choose to produce less when they could produce more?

AGGREGATE DEMAND AND BUSINESS CYCLE

We begin by considering why one business firm would choose to cut its production, then consider a market, and finally the whole economy.

Consider a business that most of us are familiar with: a restaurant. The number of meals a restaurant can produce in a day depends on the resources and technology it has available. How large is the dining room? How large and well equipped is the kitchen? How many cooks, waiters, and waitresses has it hired? In other words, the amount the restaurant can produce is determined by the same set of things that influence economic growth. If the restaurant owner wants to increase the number of meals that the restaurant can produce, she needs to increase the amount of labor, raw materials, and capital, or improve technology.

The number of meals the restaurant actually produces on any given day is determined by the number of diners who come into the restaurant. If fewer diners come, the restaurant produces fewer meals and uses fewer resources. It may reduce the number of people it employs, or it may offer fewer hours to the people that it employs. It cuts back on orders for supplies. It probably will not consider making any new investments in kitchen equipment.

There are a number of reasons that demand for meals at a restaurant might decline. It might be that diners just do not like that particular restaurant anymore. Maybe a similar restaurant opened up closer to where the diners live. These are changes that are specific to one restaurant. Often, changes in demand are specific to a particular business firm, but it is also common for changes in demand to affect an entire market.

Markets boom and decline all the time as peoples' tastes change and new products are introduced. If the decrease in demand persists over time, the number of firms in the market declines, and resources flow toward other markets where they are more valuable. When people decide they want to consume less beef, there is a decline in demand for beef, and both the price and output of beef fall. Some cattle ranchers sell off their herds and open up new businesses. Some cowboys leave the farm and find jobs in the cities.

Decreases in demand in particular markets happen all the time; they are an essential part of the process of economic growth, but sometimes demand decreases all over the economy. When the demand for goods and services all over the economy is added up it is called aggregate demand, the demand for GDP. Decreases in aggregate demand below potential output cause recessions; increases in aggregate demand beyond potential output cause inflation.

Wage Adjustments Move the Economy Back To Potential Output

Changes in aggregate demand can push the economy away from potential output, but market economies have a tendency to adjust back to potential output. This tendency to adjust back to potential output is why the unemployment rate that exists at potential output is sometimes called the natural rate of unemployment.

If aggregate demand decreases, it means that demand for goods and services has decreased in many markets at the same time. As we saw in chapter 1, decreases in demand lead to lower prices and lower production. There is, however, an important difference between a decrease in demand in a particular market and a decrease in demand in many markets at the same time. The difference is that a decrease in demand at one firm or in one market does not have much of an affect on the demand for labor, a decrease in aggregate demand does. Any single firm or market is likely to be a small part of the total demand for labor. If one firm hires less labor, it does not cause wages to decline. If one firm hires more labor, it does not cause wages to increase. If the demand for labor falls all over the economy, it can cause wages to decline. If demand for labor increases all over the economy, it can cause wages to increase. The adjustment of wages in response to a change in aggregate demand tends to push the economy back to the natural rate of output.

To see how wage adjustments push the economy back to the natural rate of output, consider a simple example where all workers get the same wage and everyone consumes only one good, lattes. The reason for this simple example is that we need to see the distinction between money (or nominal) wages and real wages. A person's nominal wage is the amount that is stated on his paycheck. A person's real wage is the quantity of goods and services that his nominal wage can purchase. Having only one good makes it easy to see the relationship between prices, nominal wages, and real wages.

We begin this example with the economy at the natural rate of output. The nominal weekly wage is $100 and the price of lattes is $4, which makes the real wage 25 lattes a week. When demand falls, the price and production of lattes fall. Say the price falls to $2. The real wage increases to 50 lattes a week. This is good for the people who are still employed, but it is bad for their employers. Employers receive a lower price for the lattes they produce and yet they are paying the same money wage. The real cost of production is up. Every person they employ for a week costs them 50 lattes instead of 25. They cut back on the number of people they employ. The increase in unemployment eventually puts downward pressure on wages. Employers reduce the nominal wages to restore the original real wage. In this case, the nominal wage would need to be reduced to $50 to restore the original real wage of 25 lattes. When the nominal wage has been reduced enough to restore the original real wage, employers are again willing to employ as many people as they did originally. Prices and nominal wages are lower, but the real wage is restored and the economy is again producing at potential output.

When aggregate demand increases, the story is reversed. The increase in demand leads to an increase in the price and quantity of lattes. As the price of lattes rises, however, the real wage falls. If we start again with a wage of $100 and then increase the price of lattes from $4 to $5, the real wage falls from 25 lattes to 20 lattes. This situation is good for employers but bad for employees. As soon as they can, workers press for wage increases to restore their purchasing power. To restore the real wage, the nominal wage has to be increased to $125. As their cost of production rises because of an increase in the money wage, employers reduce output and employment back to the original level. The economy returns to potential output.

No one, neither employees nor employers, really care about the money wage. They care about the real wage; that is, they care only about how many lattes they can have. The case of German hyperinflation illustrates just how little money wages really matter. It doesn't do any good to be a billionaire if a billion dollars won't buy a sandwich. Because employers and employees adjust the nominal wage to restore the real wage, changes in aggregate demand affect only the price level and the nominal wage in the long run. Restoring the real wage restores real output to potential output and unemployment to the natural rate of unemployment.

Summary of Business Cycles in Market Economies

To recap, there is an amount of potential output associated with the natural rate of unemployment. The amount of goods and services produced at potential output is determined by resources and technology. Potential output tends to increase over time as we accumulate more capital, discover more resources, and develop better technology. Changes in demand can knock the economy away from potential output, but the economy tends to move back toward potential output and the natural rate of unemployment as wages and prices adjust to the changes in demand. This is the basic outline of the economics of business cycles.

The basic outline of the economics of business cycles leaves us with a couple of important details to complete. First, we have not discussed the causes of changes in aggregate demand. Second, we have not discussed the details of the adjustment process. Specifically, how long does it take for the economy to move back to potential output? The story becomes more complicated at this point because economists do not all agree on the answers to these questions. There are, in fact, many different theories about how the economy as a whole, the macro-economy, functions. For example, there is the Real Business Cycle theory, the Rational Expectations theory, the New Keynesian theory, the Post-Keynesian theory, the Classical theory, the New Classical theory, and the Monetarist theory. Fortunately, these many theories can generally be grouped into two broad categories: the Classical view and the Keynesian view.

THE CLASSICAL VIEW OF BUSINESS CYCLES

The essence of the Classical view is that market economies are pretty stable. If demand decreases in one sector of the economy, another sector of the economy compensates.

Downturns in the business cycle are often characterized by layoffs, hitting managers as well as front-line employees. Corbis.

A decision by households to consume less does not decrease the total amount of demand because if people consume less, then they have more to save. If they are saving more, that means they have more to lend. More lending means lower interest rates. Lower interest rates mean more businesses are able to invest in new capital. The increase in investment makes up for the original decrease in consumer demand.

If the government spends less, then it can either tax less or borrow less. If it taxes less, that leaves more for people to consume. If it borrows less, that leaves more for private businesses to borrow and invest.

In each case, if spending falls in one place, spending increases someplace else. Likewise, if spending increases in one place, it must fall someplace else. If investment increases, government spending or consumption must fall. If consumption increases, government spending or investment must fall. At any point in time GDP is a fixed pie, the size of which is determined by resources and technology. Over time, resources and technology improve, increasing the size of the pie, but it still has to be divided between the different sectors of the economy.

In the Classical view of the economy, it is not possible, for instance, to increase the demand for goods and services by increasing government spending. If government spending increases, then the government either has to tax more or borrow more to pay for it. If it taxes more, the taxes drive down household consumption; if it borrows more, the borrowing drives up interest rates and drives down business investment.

Money in the Classical View

In the Classical view there should always be enough demand to buy the goods that can be produced, with one exception. The exception is that an unexpected decrease in the money supply can fool people into thinking that demand for goods and services is actually decreasing in all parts of the economy. When there is less money in the economy, people cannot spend as much unless each dollar circulates around the economy more quickly, that is, unless velocity increases. Classical economists think that the velocity of money is pretty stable. So, when the money supply decreases, either output has to decrease or prices have to decrease, or both. Businesses interpret falling prices as a decrease in demand. They cut production and are unwilling to employ as many people as before, so unemployment rises.

Increases in the money supply can cause increases in demand. Periods of inflation are caused by increasing the money supply more rapidly than output is increasing. The relationship between changes in the money supply and inflation can be seen in Figure 4.3, which shows the percentage change in M1 and the percentage change in the CPI. Periods of rapidly increasing prices are also periods of rapidly increasing money supply. The rapid increases in the money supply may temporarily fool people into working and producing more, but this situation does not last. When prices rise, real wages fall. People seek to increase their nominal wages to regain their old real wage. The increase in wages causes businesses to reduce employment and output. The expansion of the economy beyond potential output is only temporary and is followed by a recession in which output and the unemployment rate return to their natural rates.

If monetary policy-makers continue to increase the money supply more rapidly than potential output, people begin to expect inflation. Eventually, they start to build inflationary expectations into their wage negotiations. In order to keep fooling people, monetary policy-makers have to keep increasing the money supply and inflation more and more rapidly.

For economists who hold the Classical view, business cycle problems are largely the result of government interference in the economy. In particular, both recession and inflation are caused by poor monetary policy. Recessions

FIGURE 4.3
Changes in M1 and Changes in the CPI

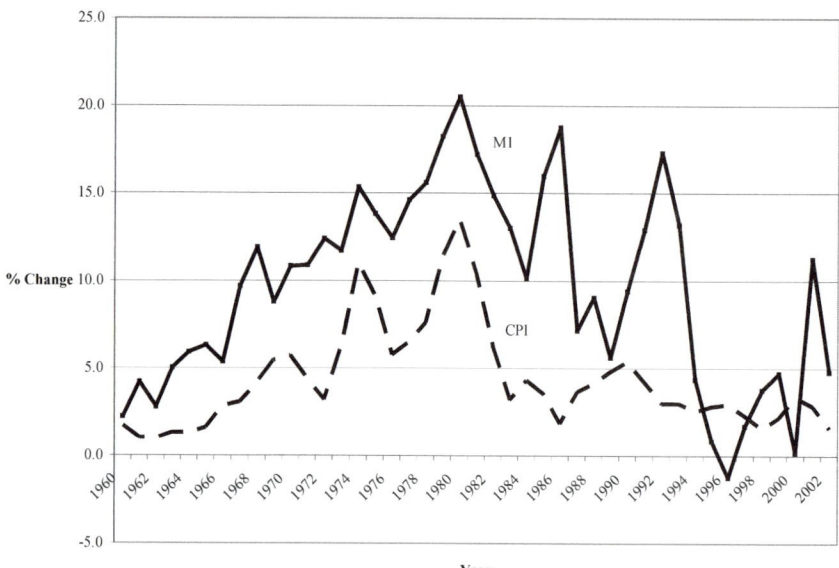

Source: Mini Historical Statistics, No. HS-36, Consumer and Gross Domestic Price Indexes: 1913 to 2002. http://www.census.gov/statab/www/minihs.html; and *Economic Report of the President, 2005,* Table B-69, Money stock and debt measures, 1959–2004.

Should Money Be as Good as Gold?

From 1900 to 1933 the United States was on a gold standard. U.S. dollars were convertible into gold at a rate of $26 per ounce. Some people think that the benefit of the gold standard was that money was backed by something of real value. Other people think that there was no benefit to having a gold standard, and that it was just something people did because that was the way it had always been done. Neither view is really correct.

The real benefit of the gold standard was that it took control of the money supply out of the hands of government authorities. Investors did not have to worry about increases in the money supply fueling inflation and destroying the value of their investments. This security was particularly important for encouraging foreign investment. Advocates of the gold standard in the late nineteenth century built their case on these benefits not on the belief that gold had been divinely created to serve as money. More recently, some less developed countries have taken a similar approach through dollarization. They have adopted the U.S. $ as their official currency, taking the control of monetary policy out of their own hands.

---

are caused by decreasing the money supply or by increasing it more slowly than potential output is increasing. Inflation is caused by increasing the money supply more rapidly than potential output is increasing.

In the Classical view, these temporary shocks to aggregate demand do not have a long-lasting affect. Prices and wages adjust quickly to return the real wage to its original level. If a recession drags on, it can be attributed to government policies, such as minimum wage laws, that keep nominal wages from adjusting.

THE KEYNESIAN VIEW OF BUSINESS CYCLES

Keynesian economics is named for the English economist John Maynard Keynes. By the time of the Great Depression, Keynes was already one of the most influential economists in the world. Keynes thought that the Classical explanation of economic downturns was inadequate. He believed that a number of things, not just decreases in the money supply, could cause demand for goods and services to decrease, and that it might take a long time for the economy to return to full employment on its own. He also believed that during severe recessions, monetary policy might not be able to increase aggregate demand and, therefore, government might have to increase aggregate demand directly by increasing government expenditures or cutting taxes.

Expectations in Keynesian Theory

Keynes emphasized the role of expectations in the economy. Businesses make decisions about how much to produce and how much new capital to purchase based on their expectations about the future. Consumers make choices about buying a car, or a house, or a refrigerator, based not just on what is happening now, but on what they think will happen in the future.

Keynes argued that changes in expectations could start recessions. The expectations that businesses have about the future are very uncertain and unstable. Expectations can change quickly. Consequently, business investment tends to be very unstable. Keynes thought that changes in investment are the most likely source of decreases in demand. However, a decrease in demand could come from any of the four parts of the economy: households, businesses, government, or the foreign sector. What is more important than where the decrease in demand comes from is what happens next.

The Expenditure Multiplier

While Classical economists argue that a decrease in demand in any one part of the economy will be offset by an increase in another part, Keynes believed that any decrease in demand could send the economy into a downward spiral. His argument went like this. The amount of goods and services households plan to buy depends on their current income and their expectations about future income. When demand decreases, businesses sell less and hire fewer people. Household income falls today, and households become pessimistic about their future incomes, so they reduce spending. That means even lower sales for other businesses, lower income, and more pessimism. And so on. This is called the multiplier process; a single fall in demand gets multiplied across the economy.

The multiplier process on a smaller scale is why people get upset when the government announces closings of military bases. People who live near the bases know that if the soldiers or sailors go away, local businesses sell fewer cars and movie tickets and restaurant meals. Lower sales mean less income for the people selling those goods, and as a result they buy fewer new homes and refrigerators and televisions.

Sticky Wages and Prices

Economists who hold the Classical view do not deny that something like a multiplier process takes place. However, in the Classical view, the decreases in demand lead to decreases in prices and wages that ultimately restore the economy to full employment. In the Keynesian view, prices and wages do not fall, or at least do not fall very quickly. When wages and prices adjust slowly or not at all to changes in aggregate demand, they are said to be sticky.

The theory of supply and demand (see chapter 1) says that when demand falls, prices fall. But Keynesians believe that in modern market economies, a number of factors might cause prices and wages to become sticky.

Explanations for price stickiness include long-term contracts, implicit contracts, and menu costs. Long-term contracts obviously leave prices fixed even as demand changes. Implicit contracts exist when firms operate according to unwritten, or implicit, agreements as well as explicit ones. Firms might be reluctant to change prices if it would be seen as violating an implicit agreement. Further, firms might be reluctant to change prices because they have to incur the costs of changing menus or catalogs.

Explanations for wage stickiness include: minimum wage legislation, long-term wage contracts, unions, and efficiency wages. Minimum wages do not inhibit increases in wages, but prevent decreases in wages. Long-term contracts prevent either increases or decreases while they are in effect. For instance, it is not unusual for salaried workers to have contract adjustments just once a year. Efficiency wages arise from the fact that firms use wages to motivate workers. Employers may be willing to pay greater than market wages to encourage greater productivity from their workers. They may be reluctant to lower wages because of the negative effect on employee morale.

Keynesians argue that wages and prices fall only if aggregate demand stays down over a long period of time. If prices do not fall, workers are reluctant to accept lower wages. If wages do not fall, the cost of production does not fall and businesses are not able to increase their production again. There is nothing to move the economy back toward full employment; it gets stuck in a depression.

Although Keynes believed that prices are sticky, he did not believe that trying to make prices less sticky would solve the problem. Because of the emphasis he placed on expectations, he thought that falling prices and wages might make matters even worse. As prices and wages fall, he believed, businesses and households become even more pessimistic about the future and even less likely to open their wallets and buy something. Thus whether wages were sticky or not, Keynes thought that it was necessary for government to take steps to increase aggregate demand to end a recession.

MONEY IN THE KEYNESIAN VIEW

Keynes did not believe that monetary policy would always be effective at increasing aggregate demand. Unlike Classical economists, he believed that changes in the money supply do not directly influence changes in spending, but instead influenced spending indirectly through changes in the interest rate. The interest rate is the price of money. When we want to spend more money than we currently have, we have to borrow. The price we pay for borrowing is the interest rate. If the supply of money increases, the price of money—the interest rate—falls. If the interest rate falls, people are willing to borrow more and spend more. If the money supply decreases, the interest rate rises. People borrow less and spend less.

Because increasing the money supply influences the economy only by encouraging borrowing, Keynes saw two places where the process could break down. First, if banks are very pessimistic about the economy, they might not be willing to make loans. Second, even if banks are willing to lend, businesses and households might not be willing to borrow if they are sufficiently pessimistic about their future incomes.

USING FISCAL POLICY TO STIMULATE THE ECONOMY

Since Keynes believed that the economy might not automatically adjust on its own, and monetary policy might be incapable of increasing demand, Keynes argued that fiscal policy is necessary to move an economy out of a depression. He suggested that when the economy is operating below full employment, an increase in government spending encourages increases in private spending, including investment. His argument rested on the importance of expectations and the multiplier effect.

Suppose government increases spending; it spends $100 million on a new highway. The increase in spending increases the incomes of owners of construction companies and construction workers by $100 million. Those people might set aside $10 million and spend $90 million of the increase in income on new cars and clothes. Their spending becomes income for other people in the automobile and textile markets, who in turn spend part of their increase in income. All over the economy, incomes rise, expectations about the future improve, and businesses again invest. The multiplier effect that Keynes believed could cause the economy to go into a downward spiral also meant that changes in government spending could have an effect on the economy much larger than the initial change.

Like the Classical view, inflation in the Keynesian view is caused by increasing the money supply more rapidly than potential output. Although the Keynesian view is that increases in aggregate demand can come from any of the sectors of the economy, an increase in demand beyond potential output cannot be sustained without an increase in the money supply. Increasing total demand means that people are trying to buy more goods and services; to do so they need more money. If the supply of money is held fixed while demand for money increases, the price of money, the interest rate, rises. The increase in the interest rate chokes off the increase in demand. An increase in aggregate demand cannot lead to inflation unless the money supply increases more rapidly than potential output.

COMMON GROUND IN KEYNESIAN AND CLASSICAL VIEWS

Although inflation in both views is ultimately the result of increasing the money supply more rapidly than potential output, the Classical and Keynesian explanations of the interest rate appear to differ. The Classical view says that interest rates are determined by the savings rate, while the Keynesian approach says that interest rates are determined by the money supply. The two views of the interest rate are reconciled by recognizing the distinction between real and nominal interest rates.

To see the difference between real interest rates and nominal interest rates, imagine this scenario. There is a stereo you want to buy for $100, but you also have the option of loaning that $100 to a friend for one year at 10 percent interest. The nominal, or agreed upon, interest rate is 10 percent. If you loan out the $100 at an interest rate of 10 percent for one year, at the end of the year you get back your $100 plus $10 more for the interest. But suppose prices increase 10 percent during the course of the year, so that the price of the stereo is $110. Your $110 buys just the same stereo, and nothing more. The real interest rate, the nominal interest rate adjusted for the price increase, on the loan was 0 percent. In other words, the real interest rate on a loan is equal to the nominal rate minus the rate of inflation.

Assume that we are initially at potential output with an interest rate of 5 percent and no inflation. Suppose the money supply increases, causing a decrease in the interest rate to 4 percent. If people are not expecting inflation, they treat the decrease in the interest rate as a decrease in the real interest rate. They borrow and spend more. But because the economy was already at potential output, the increase in the money supply eventually causes inflation. When people realize that inflation is taking place, lenders recognize that the real interest rate has fallen. They increase the nominal interest rate to compensate for the inflation. If inflation is 2 percent, the nominal interest rate will have to rise to 7 percent to return to the real rate of 5 percent. Just like workers and employers, lenders and borrowers are concerned with the real, not the nominal. As the interest rate rises, people borrow less and spend less.

In the short run, changes in the money supply can influence the real rate of interest, real output, and employment. In the long run, however, the real rate of interest is governed by the supply of saving and the demand for loanable funds. Classical economists focus on the real interest rate because they believe that people cannot be fooled for long and that the economy adjusts back toward the appropriate real interest rate and real wage rate relatively quickly. Keynesian economists focus on the money supply as the determinant of the interest rate because they think that people adjust only slowly.

What Caused the Great Depression?

The Great Depression was a defining moment in American economic history. More than a half century after it ended, economists still argue about why it happened and whether it can happen again. Keynesian economists argue that it was caused by a large decrease in consumption expenditures. There is no general agreement among Keynesians about what caused the decline in consumption expenditures, but they argue that the money supply was largely irrelevant because people were unwilling to borrow and spend no matter how low the interest rate. Classical economists argue that monetary policy was largely to blame for the Great Depression. The recession was initiated by the Federal Reserve increasing interest rates. As the economy fell further into a recession, the Fed raised interest rates again instead of lowering them. It stood by and let the money supply fall by $5 billion dollars and watched as thousands of banks failed. Recently, economists have explored the causes and consequences of the Fed's failure to halt the decrease of the money supply.

First, they examined the role of the Gold Standard in causing the Depression. Because the United States was officially committed to the Gold Standard, the money supply was tied to the quantity of gold reserves. As the economy fell into a recession, foreign investors pulled their investments out of the United States. They sold their stocks and bonds, and exchanged the dollars for gold. The Federal Reserve took the only action available to it to encourage foreign investors to keep their gold in the United States; it raised interest rates. Higher interest rates made it more attractive to keep their wealth as deposits in America. But the higher interest rate also made it more costly to borrow and decreased aggregate demand.

Second, the failure of the banking system in the United States affected more than the money supply. Banks serve an important role in the economy by bringing together lenders and borrowers. When ten thousand banks failed, the ability to bring together borrowers and lenders was markedly reduced. The decline in the banking system thus made it harder for the economy to recover from the initial recession and helps explain the slow, drawn-out recovery.

WHY WE HAVE DIFFERENT VIEWS
ABOUT THE ECONOMY

Although the debate between Keynesian and Classical economists is generally thought of as being about the economy as a whole, it is really a debate about how well individual markets work. In the basic story of the business cycle, the mechanism that returns the economy to its potential output is the adjustment of prices and wages to changes in demand. If prices and wages both fall very quickly, the economy quickly returns to its potential output. If prices and wages do not change very quickly—in particular, if firms do not want to lower their prices and workers do want to accept lower wages—then the economy gets bogged down below its potential output. The debate is fundamentally about how well markets work.

Predicting Business Cycle Movements

Many people would like to know what is going to happen to the economy in the future. Businesses do not want to make a large investment, increase hiring, or build up their inventories right before a recession. Many businesses hire economists or economic forecasting firms to tell them what is likely to happen in the future. These forecasts are built on economic theories. They generally use sophisticated statistical techniques and complex mathematical models. A less complicated approach is provided by looking at leading indicators. Leading indicators are things that tend to change before general changes in economic activity occur. They tend to increase before GNP increases and decrease before GNP decreases. The Conference Board reports an index of leading indicators that summarizes the changes in the following variables:

Average weekly hours, manufacturing

Average weekly initial claims for unemployment insurance

Manufacturers' new orders, consumer goods, and materials

Vendor performance, slower deliveries, diffusion index

Manufacturers' new orders, nondefense capital goods

Building permits, new private housing units

Stock prices, five hundred common stocks

Money supply, M2

Interest rate spread, ten-year Treasury bonds less federal funds

Index of consumer expectations

Economists like to believe they follow a scientific method. They develop theories, which are just systematic explanations of how markets work, and then they try to test their theories to see if they hold up in the real world. This approach suggests that it should be possible for one group of economists to persuade another group of economists by showing that their theory makes more sense and has more evidence to back it up. If this is the case, why do economists still disagree on whether the Classical or Keynesian view is better? The main reason is that it is difficult to test macroeconomic theories.

In a laboratory, a chemist can decide exactly which chemicals she wants to mix. She can change them exactly the way she wants and she can see and accurately measure the result. An economist is never given free reign over the economy to run controlled experiments. For example, an economist never has the option of changing the money supply a little bit while holding all other government policies constant, so that she can accurately measure the result. The economist must content herself with observations of an economy in which many things are changing simultaneously. In other words, the economist must deal with the messy facts of actual human history.

It is also worth noting that the disagreements among economists are no more unusual than disagreements in other fields of study. There is no science where everything is settled, where everyone agrees about the answer to every question. If we had a definitive and unified theory of the economy, it might be more convenient, but economics would be a lot less interesting.

Five

Business and the National Economy

After all, the chief business of the American people is business.
—Calvin Coolidge

President Coolidge spoke these words during the 1920s, but they are just as true today. In 2001 there were over 25 million businesses in the United States. More than half a million new business firms are established each year. Private businesses produced $8.5 trillion of the $10.5 trillion worth of goods and services produced in 2003 and employed 110 million of the 130 million people employed in the United States. Private businesses, regardless of their size or organization, share a common goal: to produce and sell goods and services for a profit. The profit motive drives private businesses to develop the new products and processes that increase productivity and generate economic growth.

Despite the important role that business plays in our lives, Americans have always had a love-hate relationship with business. Throughout history, many people have viewed owning their own business as a goal, yet the American people have been suspicious of big business—corporations and entrepreneurs who have been unusually successful. Those having great success in business have been labeled "robber barons" and accused of using unfair means to achieve their fortunes.

THE DIFFERENT TYPES OF BUSINESSES
IN THE UNITED STATES

The vast majority of businesses in the United States are small businesses. Ninety-nine percent of businesses employ fewer than 500 workers. More than 3 million businesses employ fewer than five people. Small businesses employ half of all American workers and create most of the new jobs. In contrast, a small number of large corporations employ thousands of people. Wal-Mart alone employs over 1.5 million people.

Starting a business requires the ability to purchase the resources necessary for production. There are two ways to obtain these funds. The owners of the business can either use their own money or they can borrow money from others. Money raised through ownership is called equity. Money raised by borrowing from others is called debt. The choices that people make about the use of debt and equity influence the legal form of organization that they use to start a business.

Proprietorships

Most small businesses are organized as proprietorships. A proprietorship is a business that is owned by an individual. An advantage of the proprietorship is that there is a very strong incentive for the business to be well managed. The person who makes the decisions is the person who gets the profits.

A disadvantage of the proprietorship is that the owner has unlimited liability for the debts of the business. Unlimited liability means that all of the assets of the owner can be claimed by creditors to pay the debts of the business. Take, for instance, the case of someone who owns a small clothing store. If the business fails and the owner is unable to pay its debts, the creditors of the business can claim not only the assets in the store to pay the debts, but the proprietor's house, car, and other personal assets as well. In other words, there is no separation between a proprietor's business assets and his personal assets when it comes to paying debts.

Another drawback of a proprietorship is that it tends to limit the amount of money a person can raise to finance the business. A proprietor may start a business with a combination of personal savings and some small loans. The loans may come from a variety of places: a bank, friends, relatives, and suppliers. Suppliers often provide credit to small businesses by not making them pay for goods at the time the goods are delivered. This type of loan is called trade credit. If a supplier delivers clothes to a store but does not make the bill due until a month later, it is just the same as if the supplier had loaned the store the money to buy the clothes.

PARTNERSHIPS

If a proprietor needs money to expand the business, one option is to form a partnership. A partnership is a business that is jointly owned by several people. A disadvantage of partnerships is that, in most partnerships, the partners are jointly responsible for all the obligations of the business. That is, they each have unlimited liability. Consider the case of two partners in a business that has assets of $1 million. The first partner has personal assets worth $500,000; the second partner has personal assets worth $200,000. If the business fails with debts of $1,600,000, the first partner can lose all the assets of the business and $400,000 of her assets even though that is twice as much as her partner loses. A partnership can put a business owner into some scary situations. One partner might take on risky debts for the business even though he does not have any personal assets to contribute to paying the debt if the company fails.

Partnerships are most common in the professional services: law firms, medical practices, accounting firms, and real estate companies. Partners in these firms tend to have a very large stake in the firm. Often prospective partners have to go through a sort of apprenticeship, in which the partners evaluate them, before they can become one of the partners.

CORPORATIONS

If a business needs a great deal of finance to start up or expand, it is likely to be organized as a corporation. Organizing a business as a corporation takes care of the problem of having to monitor the other owners of the company because each owner has only limited liability. The liability of owners of a corporation is limited to the money used to buy stock in the business. If a person spends $1,000 to buy ten shares of stock, that is the most he can lose if the company fails. Limited liability makes it easier to raise large amounts of money by selling shares of ownership to many people.

Corporations can issue common stock or preferred stock. Holders of common stock are allowed to vote on the management of the corporation, owners of preferred stock are not. In exchange for giving up control of the management of the corporation, holders of preferred stock get first claim on dividends. Dividends are the part of the corporation's profits that it pays out to its shareholders. If any dividends are paid out, preferred stockholders must receive dividends first.

A corporation has several other advantages. For example, it can sue and be sued in its own right. In the eyes of the law, the corporation is a person. Though unlike a person, the corporation can live forever. Unlike a proprie-

The skyscraper—the iconic image of the corporation. Getty Images: PhotoLink.

torship or partnership, the death of one of the owners has no effect on the continued existence of the business.

There are disadvantages to the corporate form of organization. A disadvantage of spreading out the ownership of the corporation is that it leads to a separation of ownership and control. Unlike a proprietorship or partnership, the owners do not have direct control of the corporation. Although the managers of a corporation may own some of the stock, they do not usually own all of it and therefore do not get all the benefits of actions that raise the value of the stock. Managers may even have incentives to do things that do not benefit stockholders. They may spend lavishly on corporate jets, cars, and offices that benefit themselves at the expense of stockholders. Part of this problem can be overcome with compensation schemes that tie profits to managerial actions. For example, managers may receive stock options. A simple example of a stock option is a manager having the option to buy stock next year at the price that exists this year. The manager profits from any increase in the price of the stock that occurred during the year. The threat of a takeover also reduces management misbehavior. If the managers take actions that reduce the value of the stock, someone might be able to buy enough stock to gain control of the company and replace the management.

Another disadvantage of the corporate form is that the profit of a corporation is taxed twice. First, the corporation pays a tax on its profits.

Second, shareholders pay income tax on their dividends. In contrast, the profits of a proprietorship or partnership are simply taxed as income of the owners. A final disadvantage of the corporation is that corporations are subject to greater regulatory oversight than other businesses.

Proprietorship, partnership, and corporation are the basic organizational forms of businesses, but there are other forms that mix elements of the three. Consider franchising. In a franchise agreement, one business sells to another the right to operate under its name, in exchange for a fee and royalties in sales. The franchisee owns the franchised business but must operate on the terms set out in the agreement; for instance, the franchisee might be required to buy supplies from the franchiser. Franchisers generally provide franchisees with a known product and advice on operating the business.

Another mixed form of organization is the limited partnership. In a limited partnership there are general partners who control the management of the business, and there are limited partners who have limited liability but do not have a say in the management of the business.

Organizing a Corporation

Not all corporations are big businesses, but all of the biggest businesses are corporations. Although most businesses are proprietorships, most sales are by corporations; see Table 5.1. Corporations can become very large because they can raise large amounts of capital.

The initial investment funds for a corporation usually come from a relatively small number of people. Such corporations are called "private" or "closely held" corporations. Often if the company is successful, it "goes public." Going public means that the corporation sells shares to anyone who wants to buy, and sales prices are listed on a stock exchange. Not all companies go public. Cargill, an agribusiness firm with over $60 billion in

TABLE 5.1
Number of Businesses and Sales, 2001

Organizational Form	Number (1,000s)	Sales Receipts (billions $s)
Proprietorship	18,338	1,017
Partnership	2,132	2,569
Corporation	5,136	19,308

Source: U.S. Census Bureau, *Statistical Abstract of the United States, 2004–2005*, No. 716; Number of Returns, Receipts, and Net Income by Type of Business: 1980 to 2001.

revenue in 2004, has remained a privately held corporation for over one hundred years. The benefit of going public is that sales of newly issued stock to the public provide a way of obtaining a large amount of new funds for investment. In addition, the original investors experience an increase in their wealth that they can, if they choose, easily convert to cash.

Google is a good example of corporate evolution. Google Inc. was formed almost by accident. Its founders hoped to make a profit by developing a better Internet search engine, but they started to consider building their own business only when they were unable to sell their technology to Yahoo or other existing firms. One of the first people the Google guys talked to about investing in a new business was a cofounder of Sun Microsystems, who promptly wrote out a check for $100,000 to "Google Inc." But there was not yet a Google Inc. The check sat in a locked desk while the Google guys did the paperwork to establish a corporation. Google Inc. was formed in September 1998, and its shares were held by a relatively small group of investors.

In 2004, Google announced that it would go public; it would issue new stock tradable on stock exchanges. Companies go public through an "initial public offering," often abbreviated as IPO. In its initial public offering, Google stock sold for $85 per share. On its first day of trading it closed at over $100, making the company worth about $27 billion. Each of the cofounders had stock worth about $3.8 billion. The initial public offering raised a little over $1 billion in new funds for the business.

Initial public offerings are carried out by investment banks, which underwrite the offering. Underwriting an initial public offering means that the investment bank buys the stock that will be made available to the public and then resells the new stocks to the public. The investment bank makes its profit from the difference between what it pays the corporation for the stock and what it is able to charge the public.

Investment banks underwrite bond issues in the same way. Bonds are a form of debt finance. The firm that issues a bond has an obligation to make payments at the times and in the amounts stated on the bond. Failure to make the stated payments puts the firm in default and it can be forced into bankruptcy.

Investment banks operate very differently than commercial banks. Commercial banks take savings and checking accounts and make loans for homes, cars, or some business investments. Investment banks do not have depositors and do not make loans. Despite different methods of operation, both commercial banks and investment banks serve the same basic function in the economy: They move funds from savers to businesses.

THE STOCK MARKET

Again, once a company goes public, its shares can be bought and sold on a stock exchange. While an initial public offering brings funds into the business, the purchase of a share on the stock exchange brings no additional money to the business. The money paid for the stock simply goes to the person who owned the stock before and sold it. Although money does not go to the corporation when its stock is traded, stock exchanges are very important for promoting investment. People would be much less willing to purchase any stock if they did not know they could easily sell it later.

What is commonly called the "stock market" is actually a number of different stock exchanges. The largest and most well known is the New York Stock Exchange on Wall Street. The New York Stock Exchange is very modern and very old-fashioned at the same time. It is connected to the world with thousands of phones and hundreds of miles of cable, yet trading takes place face-to-face on the floor of the exchange. Other stock markets include the American Stock Exchange, also on Wall Street, regional exchanges, and Nasdaq, which is an electronic market and not located in any single place. Nasdaq lists over five thousand stocks and is the market for many high-tech stocks.

When a person wants to buy or sell stock, he contacts a broker, giving an order to buy or sell. The broker forwards the message to her representative at the exchange, who makes the purchase or sale. In the case of Nasdaq, stockbrokers interact through an electronic network rather than on the floor of an exchange.

The price of stock can be influenced by many different things, but ultimately the price of stock reflects the beliefs of people all over the world about the value of the business. Poor sales figures or any other report that reflects poorly on the value of a business tends to lower the price of its stock.

Often we are less interested in the price of the stock of a single business and more interested in what is happening to stock prices generally. On any one day, some stock prices go up while others go down. The problem of describing the simultaneous movements of many different stock prices is the same problem that we face when we try to describe the price level for the entire economy. We solve the problem by using the same technique as we used to compute the price indices in chapter 2. Just as we use the CPI and PPI to describe prices for the entire economy, we compute price indices to describe overall changes in stock prices. The price of the entire market basket of stocks is compared to its price in a base year. The well-known stock indices include: the Dow Jones Industrial Average, the Standard and Poor's

500, and the Nasdaq Composite Index. In addition to stock indices, people describe stock market activity in terms of the ratio of buyers to sellers, the ratio of gainers to losers, and the volume of trade.

WHY SOME BUSINESSES ARE VERY LARGE

The corporate form of organization and stock markets make it possible to have large-scale businesses. But the existence of these institutions does not explain why some businesses are large and others are small. Differences in the size of businesses arise mainly because of economies of scale and economies of scope.

Economies of scale exist when it is possible to achieve a lower average cost of production with a larger business establishment than with a smaller one. For example, producing cars on an automated assembly line lowers the cost per car, but only if the business produces thousands of cars in the same place. Producing only one hundred cars on an assembly line creates very high average costs because the entire cost of the assembly line is spread over the small number of cars.

Economies of scope exist when a single business can produce a variety of goods or services more cheaply than other firms can produce each one separately. Wal-Mart provides a good example of economies of scope. In recent years, Wal-Mart expanded beyond traditional department store offerings into the retailing of groceries at the "Super Wal-Mart" stores. At its "super" stores, Wal-Mart is able to offer both lines of products more cheaply than other firms can offer either one separately.

Sears provides an earlier example of economies of scope in retailing. Sears began as a mail order watch business. It sold watches out of catalogs. Sears found it could profit by expanding the variety of goods in its catalog. In the first decades of the twentieth century, the Sears catalog even included houses. Every part of a house would be delivered by train and assembled at the lot of the buyer. Many of these houses still stand today.

Economies of scope arise from what is called the core competency of a business. The core competency is the thing the business does best. The core competency of a business is not always obvious. The core competency of Wal-Mart is not just stocking department store goods, but discount retailing. The core competency of Sears was not watches, but catalog sales.

We sometimes see both large and small businesses in a market, despite economies of scale and scope. Anheuser-Busch is America's largest brewer. Its brewery in St. Louis is capable of producing 2.6 million twelve-ounce cans of beer a day. Its bottling machine can fill and cap 1,100 bottles per minute. Beer is also made in brew pubs, which produce just enough beer to serve the customers of the pub. The cost of brewing twelve ounces of beer is considerably more at the brew pub, but the brew pub may still be profitable. It is profitable because some people are willing to pay a higher price for what they believe is greater quality and variety.

Economies of scale and scope can make very large businesses profitable. But economies of scale and scope have limits. Despite the economies of scale in automobile manufacture, we do not see only one big automobile firm. The limits to economies of scale come from organizational problems. Large corporations face the managerial problems of information, authority, and incentives.

A sole proprietor with no employees does not face any of these problems. The proprietor has all the information available to the business, sole authority to make decisions, and the incentive to act in the best interest of the business. If the proprietor hires employees, he faces managerial problems. If the business has a small number of employees working alongside the proprietor, managerial problems are minimal. When a business has thousands, tens of thousands, or even hundreds of thousands of employees, managerial problems are significant. A large business needs professional managers. A large business needs organizational systems to indicate how information is to flow and who has the authority to make decisions.

Beer bottles on an assembly line. Getty Images: PhotoLink.

COMPETITION AND PRICING

Through economies of scale and scope big businesses can lower the cost of production of some goods, but people question whether big businesses actually use their size to charge prices that are higher than a smaller, less powerful firm would. However, the ability to raise prices depends on the degree of competition that the business faces in its market, not upon the size of the business. Big businesses are not necessarily monopolies, and monopolies are not necessarily big businesses.

A monopoly is a single business that supplies a whole market. By reducing supply, a monopoly may be able to drive up the price and thereby increase profits.

The ability to reduce supply and drive up the price is called market power, or monopoly power. For a business to have market power, it has to be the case that consumers do not think that there are close substitutes for what the business produces. The more substitutes there are for a product, the less market power a business has.

In agricultural markets, many farms produce similar products, so no single farmer has influence over the total supply or price. The current market price of wheat, or corn, or soybeans is the result of people from all over the world buying and selling the commodity. Each farmer who agrees to sell at the current market price accepts that price; no farmer has influence over the price. Suppose the current market price of wheat is $1.25 per bushel. If a farmer wants $1.30 per bushel, he does not agree to sell at the current price. Moreover, if he tried to sell even one bushel at $1.30, no one would buy it from him because there are many other farmers who are selling an identical bushel of wheat for $1.25.

Now consider the near-absolute market power of the business that made the first ballpoint pens. When the ballpoint pen was introduced by the Reynolds International Pen Company in October 1945, the pens sold for $12.50. Each pen cost 80 cents to manufacture. Reynolds made profits as high as $500,000 per month. $12.50 in 1945 is equivalent to about $110 in 2004. Most people today would consider $110 quite a lot for a ballpoint pen. Yet for many people in 1945, the ballpoint was worth it. Some consumers considered ballpoints a great improvement over the nearest substitutes—impermanent pencils and messy fountain pens.

Few markets are characterized by the extremes of many perfect substitutes or virtually no substitutes. Most goods have substitutes that are close, but not perfect, substitutes. Consider the case of the market for restaurant meals. If your favorite restaurant increased its prices by a little bit, you would probably still eat there about as often as before. Other restaurants do not have perfect substitutes for what you eat at your favorite place. If a business can increase its prices without losing all its customers, it has some market power. On the other hand, even if other meals are not perfect substitutes for your favorite restaurant, you would go less often if its prices doubled. There is a limit to its market power. Most businesses have some control over price, but not too much. They exist in between the extremes of perfect competition and monopoly.

Most businesses strive to become more like a monopoly. Businesses advertise to convince consumers that there is only one product that will satisfy their specific needs—their product. Porsche's slogan is a classic example: "Porsche. There is no substitute."

Monopoly from Innovation

A sure way to achieve a monopoly, at least in the short run, is to produce something new and different. Pursuit of monopoly profits is what generates new and cheaper goods and services for consumers. As the economist Joseph Schumpeter phrased it: "The fundamental impulse that sets the capitalist engine in motion comes from the new consumers' goods, the new methods of production or transportation, the new markets, the new forms of industrial organization that the capitalist enterprise creates." Schumpeter makes clear that innovation is not just about creating new products or new machines, it's also about finding new markets and new methods of organization. Development of the multidivisional firm and franchising as methods of organization were as innovative as the automated assembly line.

We tend to focus on the big innovations and entrepreneurs: Eli Whitney, Francis Cabot Lowell, Andrew Carnegie, Henry Ford, Alfred Sloan, Sam Walton, and Bill Gates. But many businesses carry out the same basic function in the economy on a much smaller scale. The person who brings a new store or restaurant to a town creates something new and valuable even if the business does not become the next McDonald's.

Monopoly profits from innovation are attractive but hard to hang on to. Recall the case of the Reynolds pen business. By the end of 1946, just over a year after the introduction of the ballpoint, there were over a hundred companies selling different ballpoint pens. By 1948 the price of a pen had fallen below a dollar, and by the 1950s the price was under twenty-five cents. By being first in the market with a product that people wanted, Reynolds made huge profits, but these extraordinary profits did not last because there was nothing to stop other business from copying the idea; there was no barrier to entry. To maintain high profits, the business must either find a way to prevent new entrants or it must continue to innovate.

Business Failure in a Market Economy

Many of the greatest entrepreneurs failed before they succeeded. Henry Heinz's pickle company went bankrupt before his ketchup company made a fortune. The Ford Motor company was Henry Ford's second try at an automobile company; his first, the Detroit Automobile Company, failed in 1900. Of course, not all successful entrepreneurs failed first. Bill Gates formed Microsoft when he was twenty-two. But those who failed first are more representative. Each entrepreneur thinks he has what consumers want when he introduces a new product or a new method of production, but the only way to find out is to try it. Trying and failing are important parts of economic progress.

Times of rapid business formation also tend to be times of rapid business failure because most new businesses fail within a few years. Survival of the fittest is at work in the market. The life of a business in a market economy is a constant competition for scarce resources. The criterion for survival is producing what people want at the lowest possible price.

Entrepreneurs who survive recreate the evolutionary process within their businesses. Thomas Edison is known for his emphasis on the importance of experimentation and failure. Robert W. Johnson of Johnson & Johnson made clear the central role of experimentation with the phrase "Failure is our most important product." Sam Walton, founder of Wal-Mart, regarded himself not as a great visionary, but as someone who was willing to try things, throw out what did not work, and expand on what did.

Introducing a new product, or a new process, or moving into a new market requires a leap of faith. The entrepreneur has to make her investment now, but her payoff comes in the future. The fact that the payoff from investment comes in the future adds an element of risk to decision-making.

INVESTING IN THE FUTURE

Entrepreneurs must compare payoffs in the future to expenditures now. Sometimes the comparison is simple. Everyone prefers $100 today to $100 one year from now. Money in the future is not worth as much as money now. Money in the future is worth less than money now because there are uses for the money in the meantime. Forgoing money today has an opportunity cost.

Instead of making an investment in the business, the entrepreneur could use the money to purchase a certificate of deposit, a Treasury bill, or some other asset that would pay a known rate of interest. The opportunity cost of using the money for investment is the interest that could have been earned.

Suppose the current market interest rate is 5 percent. The entrepreneur knows that if she has $100 today, she can loan it out at 5 percent interest. Next year she would have $100 + (100 × .05) = $100(1 + .05) = $105. It must then be true that $105 a year from now is worth just $100 now.

Now suppose the current interest rate is 8 percent. A business is considering the purchase a new piece of equipment. The cost of the equipment is $1,000. The piece of equipment is expected to have a payoff of $1,050 a year from now. The value today of $1,050 a year from now is $1,050/(1 + .08) = $972. This means that $972 is the most the business should be willing to spend on the investment; otherwise it would be better to make a loan at the market rate of interest. The entrepreneur should not undertake the investment in new plant and equipment.

This method of comparing sums of money is called finding the present value of the future payments. Calculating the present value answers the question: Would we be better off spending money on a business investment or collecting interest on it? The interest rate determines the present value of a future payoff. When the interest rate is 6 percent, an investment must pay at least $106 next year to be worth a $100 investment now. If the interest rate rises to 10 percent, the investment must pay at least $110 next year to be worth spending $100 now. When interest rates rise, investment falls because investments with lower rates of return are no longer profitable.

In addition to considering the present value of the future payoff, the entrepreneur must consider the effects of inflation. If the entrepreneur expects prices to rise in the future, a future payoff from investment is worth less today.

Similarly, the entrepreneur must consider the likelihood that she has misjudged the market and that the expected payoff will not materialize at all. An entrepreneur uses the best information available to form expectations about the payoffs of investment, but no one can foresee the future with 100 percent accuracy. If consumer expectations about the economy decline and demand falls, or prices of inputs increase, an investment can very quickly go from looking like a good idea to looking like a bad idea. Investment is encouraged by economic stability, which reduces the uncertainty of future payoffs.

BUSINESSES AND THEORIES
OF THE BUSINESS CYCLE

Chapter 4 examined two approaches to explaining business cycle movements. In the Keynesian view, businesses play a prominent role in initiating and perpetuating business cycles because investment by businesses is the most unstable part of demand for goods and services and because business pricing decisions may prevent recovery.

Keynesian economists emphasize economic expectations. It is clear from the previous section that investment decisions made by firms depend upon forecasts about future payoffs. Forecasts of future payoffs, in turn, depend upon expectations about the future level of demand and expectations about inflation.

Keynesian economists also believe that once the economy starts into a recession, it does not recover quickly because businesses are reluctant to lower their prices in response to a fall in demand. A business cycle may be perpetuated because of so-called sticky prices.

One of the biggest areas of disagreement between the Classical and Keynesian accounts is how sticky prices are. Most Keynesian economists argue that prices are pretty sticky. Classical economists argue that prices are pretty flexible. Some prices are clearly very flexible: Prices of stocks and commodities change constantly throughout the trading day. But most prices do not to fluctuate throughout the day. Yet, as discussed above, most businesses do have some control over price. Studies of price changes find that businesses change their prices only infrequently, seldom more often than every three months, but often at least once per year. It is difficult to assess whether or not this degree of stickiness in prices is sufficient to prevent recovery from recessions.

In the Classical view, businesses do not play an explicit role in business cycles. Recessions come from a decline in our ability to produce goods and services or from mismanagement of the money supply. Classical emphasis on monetary policy, however, implies a behind-the-scenes role for business. We saw above how business investment depends on the interest rate. In the short run, the Federal Reserve may be able to alter the interest rate through monetary policy (see chapter 7). If the Federal Reserve responds to a recession by successfully lowering the interest rate, investment increases. The increase in investment increases output back toward the economy's potential.

Six

Households and the
National Economy

In 2002, there were 111,278,000 households in the United States with an average size of 2.57 people per household. A household can include just one person, a couple (married or not), single adults with children, or couples (married or not) with children. Sixty-nine percent of these households, or 75,596,000, were families with an average size of 3.19 persons per household. A family is a group of people related by birth, marriage, or adoption living in the same household. Half of families earned more than $51,680 in 2002 and half earned less.

Along with businesses, households are at the foundation of a market economy. Households own the resources necessary to produce goods and services. Some businesses own capital and land, but households own those businesses directly or through shares of stock. How households choose to use their resources influences both the long-run growth and the short-run fluctuations of the economy. Ultimately households decide what gets produced in a market economy because businesses survive only by providing the goods and services that households want to buy.

HOUSEHOLDS TRADE INPUTS FOR INCOME

A household in a market economy obtains income by selling the resources it owns. It sells its land, or it sells the use of its land by renting it. It receives interest or profits in exchange for letting businesses use its savings. It sells the labor of household members for wages or salaries. By far the most important of the resources of households is labor. Over 70 percent of household income is compensation for labor.

Pay Is Based on the Value of What a Person Produces

Households supply labor and businesses demand it. Businesses hire labor to produce the goods and services they sell. A business hires a person if the additional revenue it expects to gain from hiring the person outweighs the additional cost of hiring. The revenue that a person's labor contributes to a business depends upon the productivity of the person and the value of the good or service produced. If a firm's product sells for $1 per unit, and hiring another person increases production by ten units per hour, then the new hire adds $10 per hour to the firm's revenue. The firm hires if compensation is $10 per hour or less.

Firms get high profits if labor compensation is low, but firms cannot pay people less than what they add to revenue. Firms cannot pay very low wages for the same reason that they cannot charge very high prices for their products. Competition determines prices for products and prices for resources. If the labor market is competitive, people do not accept wages that are less than what they add to revenue.

Suppose a firm offers compensation of $7 per hour to a chemical engineer. The engineer turns the firm down, saying: "I can do better somewhere else." A sixteen-year-old with no job experience is likely to accept an offer of $7 per hour. Teenagers earn less than engineers because the value of what teens have to sell is less. The value of labor depends partly on a person's productivity and partly upon the market value of a firm's product.

The productivity of labor differs from one person to another. The productivity of labor depends in part on choices made within a household. A household can increase the productivity of its labor by choosing to invest in human capital. Human capital is any learning that increases productivity. Productivity goes up with work experience and formal education.

Table 6.1 shows the effects of work experience and education on income. Regardless of the level of education, there is an experience premium. A high school dropout with thirty years of experience earns $5,000 more per year than a dropout with no experience. The impact of investing in formal education is more striking. The average college graduate earns more in her twenties than a high school graduate with thirty years of work experience.

The productivity of labor also depends in part on luck. Lance Armstrong was born with a larger-than-normal heart and blood vessels that make his labor as an athlete unusually productive. Other people are born with a

TABLE 6.1
Education, Experience, and Average Earnings, 2001

Education level	Ages: 25–34	35–44	45–54	55–64	Estimated lifetime earnings
High school dropout	25,316	29,177	29,779	30,798	1,150,698
High school graduate	31,565	36,922	38,235	38,802	1,455,253
Some college, no degree	35,816	43,469	46,140	47,158	1,725,822
Associate's	38,512	45,594	48,253	47,778	1,801,373
Bachelor's	51,645	67,471	68,509	69,092	2,567,174
Master's	60,738	77,622	77,676	80,271	2,963,076
Doctorate	71,903	110,564	101,110	114,681	3,982,577

Source: Federal Reserve Bank of Dallas, 2004 Annual Report, *What D'Ya Know: Lifetime Learning in Pursuit of the American Dream.*

natural aptitude for science, art, or business that makes them more productive than others who work equally hard.

The value of labor to a firm is related to the market value of a firm's product. If the price of what someone produces goes up, the value of their labor goes up. If the price of what someone produces goes down, the value of their labor goes down. In other words, the value of a household's resources depends in part on the choices that all the other households are making about the goods and services they consume. One hundred years ago, even extraordinary skill at professional sports was not a path to great wealth because fans were not willing to pay a great deal to watch sports and because advertisers were not willing to pay a great deal to sponsor sports. Being able to repair a VCR was a valuable skill that lost its value when it became cheaper to buy a new VCR than to fix an old one. The importance of the worker's contribution to a firm's revenue is apparent in the starting salaries of college graduates. In 2004, starting salaries for chemical engineering and computer science majors averaged over $49,000, while starting salaries for psychology and journalism majors averaged under $30,000.

Households can increase their ownership of resources by saving (forgoing consumption today) and investing (in human capital or in financial or physical assets), but each household's ownership of resources is partly due to luck. People who are born into a family that has saved, accumulated wealth, and passed it down from generation to generation have more resources to sell. The lucky have higher incomes than those who have not been so fortunate.

TOTAL COMPENSATION INCLUDES WAGES AND BENEFITS

Note that employers are concerned not only with the wage, but with the total cost of hiring a worker. In addition to the wage, employers have to pay payroll taxes for the people they employ. Employers may also pay for insurance or for private pension plans. Non-wage compensation has become a larger part of total compensation over the last thirty years. Because households do not pay taxes on most non-wage compensation, they can be more valuable to the employee than the cash. Reports of declining real wages often overlook the non-wage part of compensation.

Average hourly wages in real terms (1982 dollars) fell from $8.42 an hour in 1970 to $8.24 an hour in 2002. Over the same period, private insurance and pension contributions increased from 6.7 percent of total compensation to 11.3 percent of compensation. Contributions to payroll taxes rose from 3.8 percent of compensation to 6.0 percent of compensation. Overall, real compensation per hour increased 45 percent.

The Minimum Wage

The United States has had a federal minimum wage since 1938. The current minimum wage is $5.15. Employers are not to pay less than that wage, though there are some exceptions to the rule. Increases in the minimum wage receive a great deal of positive attention from labor interests and negative attention from business interests. However, changing the minimum wage by a little is unlikely to either save the poor or wreck the economy. Of the 72 million people employed in 2002, about 3 percent were paid a wage at or below the minimum wage. Of the 3 percent, half were under the age of 24, and one-fourth were under the age of 19. Most minimum-wage workers do not stay in minimum wage jobs for long—usually less than a year. Opponents of a minimum wage argue that raising the price of labor reduces employment. Proponents argue that the effect on employment is small and is outweighed by the increase in income to the poor. Empirical studies find contradictory results, though generally they have found that small increases do not have a large impact on employment. Any increase in unemployment from an increase in minimum wage is among young people with little job experience, who are the people who have the most to gain from working. Of course, a large enough increase in the minimum wage must decrease employment. If this were not true, there would be no reason to stop at $5 or $6 an hour when we could just as easily pass a law to require $50 an hour.

INCOME INEQUALITY AND POVERTY

Because households differ from one another in the amount and value of resources they can sell, income is not equally distributed. Figure 6.1 shows the division of income in the United States in 2002. It divides households into five groups of equal size, called quintiles. The bottom one-fifth of the population includes the households with the lowest incomes, the second fifth includes the households with the next lowest incomes, and so on. The top fifth has the highest incomes. The top fifth receives almost half of all household income. The bottom fifth receives less than 5 percent of all household income.

In 2003, 58.3 million people in the U.S. lived at or below the poverty line. The concept of a poverty line was developed in the 1960s by Mollie

FIGURE 6.1
Distribution of Income in the United States, 2002

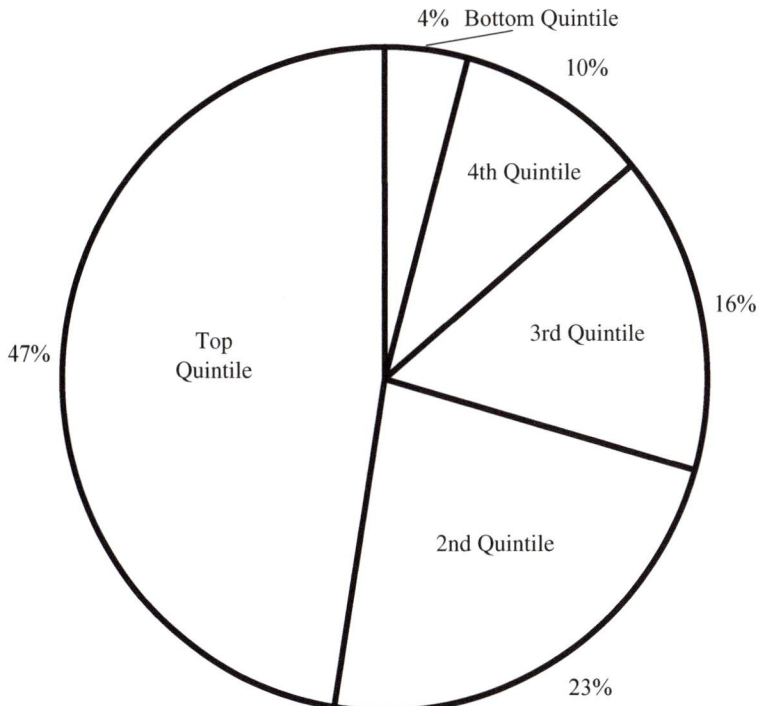

Source: U.S. Census Bureau, *Statistical Abstract of the United States, 2004–2005;* Table 672. Share of Aggregate Income Received by Each Fifth and Top 5 Percent of Families: 1980 to 2002.

Orshansky. She estimated the minimum amount of money that it took to buy a nutritionally adequate diet and then multiplied that number by three because households spent about one-third of income on food. The poverty line rises as the number of people in the household rises because more food is needed. In 2003 the poverty line for a family of four was $18,810.

Statistics on the number of people in poverty are usually based on earnings in the labor and other resource markets. These statistics do not usually include benefits from government programs for low-income households. When benefits from government programs are included, the number of people in poverty drops by almost half, to 30.9 million.

At any point in time, income is unequally distributed. Poverty, however, is not a permanent condition for most households. Most people begin their working lives at the lower end of the distribution and work their way up as they accumulate human capital and work experience. A study using the University of Michigan's Panel Survey of Income Dynamics found that 95 percent of people in the bottom quintile in 1975 were no longer there sixteen years later. Similarly, the Treasury Department found that 86 percent of those in the bottom fifth in 1979 had moved up by 1988.

DISCRIMINATION AND EARNINGS

Experience and education do not explain all income inequality in the United States Table 6.2 shows income and poverty rates by race in 2001. The highest income and lowest poverty group is Asian and Pacific Islanders, followed by Whites. Hispanics and Blacks have the lowest incomes and highest poverty rates. Poverty is higher among households headed by women

TABLE 6.2
Income, Poverty, and Education by Race, 2001

Race	Median Household Income	Percentage Below Poverty Line	Percentage with College Degree
White	$45,086	7.8%	26.6%
Black	29,026	21.5	15
Asian and Pacific Islander	52,626	7.4	47.5
Hispanic	33,103	19.7	11.1

Sources: U.S. Census Bureau, *Statistical Abstract of the United States, 2004–2005*, Table No. 690, Families below Poverty Level by Selected Characteristics, 2002; Table No. 665, Money Income of Households—Percent Distribution by Income Level, Race, and Hispanic Origin, in Constant (2002) Dollars: 1980 to 2002; Table No. 212, Educational Attainment by Race and Hispanic Origin: 1960 to 2003.

as compared to households headed by men. In addition, in 2002 the median income for a man was $29,238 and for a woman was $16,812. The differences in median incomes and poverty rates may reflect differences in the value of household resources, or they may reflect discrimination.

Discrimination in the labor market can come in several ways. A person can be discriminated against by not being interviewed or hired for a job because of race or gender. A person can be discriminated against by not being promoted because of race or gender. A person can be discriminated against by being paid a lower wage than someone else because of race or gender. A person can be discriminated against by being excluded from training necessary for a particular job.

Historically, race and gender discrimination were open and supported by the law. For instance, many employers—including school districts—had policies against employing married women. Some colleges refused to admit either women or minorities, which prevented them from obtaining the education necessary to enter certain professions.

Since the 1960s the federal government has actively opposed discrimination in education and employment. To say that discrimination is no longer legally allowed does not mean that it no longer takes place. A recent study found that a résumé bearing a typically African-American name was less likely to receive a positive response from an employer than the same résumé with a name that was typically Caucasian.

Although discrimination persists, the accumulation of human capital is the clearest path out of poverty, regardless of race or gender. Refer again to Table 6.1, which shows the average educational attainment for each racial group. Within each group, people with more education earn more. Groups with higher educational attainment also have higher incomes and lower poverty rates. (An exception is that blacks have lower income and higher poverty than Hispanics, despite having a higher average educational attainment.)

HOUSEHOLD CONSUMPTION AND SAVINGS

In Table 6.1, income rises with education, age, and work experience. Earnings peak for the 55 to 65 age group. After retirement, incomes fall. We can think of our incomes over the course of our lifetimes as looking like a hill. When we are young and inexperienced it is low; we are at the bottom of the hill. As we accumulate human capital, our incomes rise until we reach the peak of the hill. When we retire, we move down the other side of the hill.

Households expect incomes to vary in this way over the life cycle, and they try to use borrowing and saving to spread out consumption over time.

Parents, child, dog, house: the "typical" American household. Getty Images: Borland/ PhotoLink.

If you borrow now, you have to reduce your consumption in the future in order to pay back the loan. If you save now, you can consume more in the future when you get your money back with interest. Savings may be precautionary: You save in case you get sick or laid off and are unable to work. People also save for specific purchases: the down payment on a house or for children's college education.

When we are young we borrow in order to consume more than our limited incomes allow us to. We count on having higher earnings in the future with which to pay back our debt. During middle age we pay back the debts of our youth and accumulate savings for our retirement. In retirement we draw down our savings. The process is called "consumption smoothing." Instead of consuming very little when we are young or old and consuming a lot when we are middle-aged, we spread our consumption more evenly across time by borrowing and saving.

The sum of household savings, business savings, and government savings during a year is called national savings in the national income and product accounts (described in chapter 2). Household savings is the part of household income that is not taken in taxes or spent on consumption. Some households save more than they borrow and others borrow more than they save. The same is true for business. Overall, the household sector is a net source of savings and the business sector is a net borrower.

When government revenue exceeds government expenditure so that the budget is in surplus, the government has positive savings. When government spending exceeds revenues so that the budget is in deficit, the government has negative savings. In recent years the government sector has had negative savings and has been a net borrower as the federal government runs large deficits.

THE DECLINING SAVINGS RATE

Currently the household savings rate (savings as a percentage of disposable personal income) is the lowest it has been since the 1930s. Figure 6.2 shows the savings rate for the United States from 1959–2004. After rising from the 1960s to the mid-1980s, the savings rate declined. By the early 2000s it was around 1 percent of personal disposable income. The

FIGURE 6.2
Savings as a Percent of Personal Disposable Income, 1959–2004

Source: Economic Report of the President, 2005; TABLE B-30, Disposition of personal income, 1959–2004.

decline in the savings rate is a source of concern because lower savings mean higher interest rates and less investment.

Many explanations are offered for the decline in the savings rate: an increase in wealth, an increase in productivity, an increase in available credit, and a change in tastes. The explanations do not contradict each other; each may contribute.

If the wealth of households increases, they may save less out of current income. The period of declining savings coincides with, first, a boom in the stock market and, second, a boom in the real estate market. The increase in the price of assets made people wealthier. If households believe that the increase in their wealth is permanent, they do not need to save as much now in order to pay for the things that they want to consume in the future. It's like waking up one morning and finding that someone dropped $100,000 on your doorstep. You are tempted to say: "I don't have to save as much this year as I thought I did." There is evidence that this has been a large part of the story of declining savings rates. Most of the decline in savings is among the wealthiest 20 percent of households. Because these households hold the most wealth, they are most affected by the booms in the stock and real estate markets.

If productivity increases, households expect wages and incomes to increase as well. Productivity rose rapidly beginning in the mid-1990s. If households think their incomes will continue to rise, they are comfortable saving less and consuming more now. To understand why, consider the behavior of medical students and law school students. They often accumulate large student debts while they are in their twenties. They decide to take on the debt because they have high expectations about future income and ability to repay.

If household access to credit increases, households are able to consume more than in the past. In particular, access to credit cards and credit card debt have soared since the early 1980s. Additionally, Fed chairman Alan Greenspan recently expressed concern about the way households increased current consumption by accessing home equity loans and lines of credit. The increase in access to credit is blamed for the rising rate of consumer bankruptcy.

If people's tastes change, it may change households' decisions about savings. If people today are interested in immediate gratification, they are unwilling to postpone consumption and so save less. This explanation does not have much evidence to support it. The evidence that the decline in savings occurred mainly among the wealthiest 20 percent is not consistent with a change in preferences about consumption across all of society.

The argument that currently has the most evidence to support it is the argument that people decreased their savings out of their disposable income because of an increase in their wealth. Thus whether or not savings is declining depends on how savings is defined. National income and product accounting defines savings as that part of current income that is not consumed. Households define savings as the change in their wealth. They had good reason to feel that they were wealthier. The stock of wealth of the average household is up. From 1992 to 2001 the real median net worth (in 2001 dollars) of American families increased from $230,500 to $395,500, and the mean net worth increased from $61,300 to $86,100.

WHAT DO HOUSEHOLDS CONSUME?

The preferences of household members and decision-makers, in combination with the constraint of household income, determine household consumption. One household chooses to buy a big-screen TV. Another chooses to spend an equivalent amount on books and music. Most households consume a wide variety of goods.

While the consumption of a particular household is largely determined by the tastes and preferences of the particular people in the household, average household consumption has changed considerably over time. In the early nineteenth century, most households spent nearly 100 percent of income on food, clothing, and shelter. In 1929, over 40 percent of household spending was on food and clothing alone. By the late 1990s, less than 25 percent of household spending was on food and clothing. From 1929 to 2000, spending on medical care rose from 4 percent to 17 percent, and spending on recreation increased from 5.7 to 8.4 percent.

Household decisions about consumption figure prominently in Keynesian explanations of how business cycle movements get prolonged (see chapter 4). If household incomes fall, they reduce consumption, reducing aggregate demand even more, sending the economy into a downward spiral. If household incomes rise, they increase consumption, increasing aggregate demand, fueling further expansion.

Most household spending is regarded as consumption in national income and product accounting, but recall from chapter 2 that new residential construction is part of investment. New residential construction is a leading indicator in business cycles because if households expect a downturn, then they invest in less new housing.

THE CHANGING AMERICAN HOUSEHOLD

Over the past two hundred years, the very nature of the household in the American economy has changed. Households in the nineteenth century were responsible for many of the economic activities that are carried out in markets today.

Before the mid-nineteenth century, a wider variety of economic activity took place within households than is the case today. The vast majority of households were rural and engaged in agriculture. Households participated in markets and directed part of their production to markets, but specialization and division of labor had not developed to a great extent. Households produced for themselves many of the goods that are now purchased through markets.

An outstanding picture of the household in early America is provided by the historian Laurel Thatcher Ulrich in *A Midwife's Tale*. The book is based on the diary of Martha Ballard, who lived in Maine in the late 1700s and early 1800s. Her household was upper-middle-class by the standards of the time. Both she and her husband had valuable skills: she as a midwife, he as a surveyor. Although they earned income by selling their services to others, they also grew much of their own food, chopped their own wood for fuel and building, spun their own thread, weaved their own cloth, sewed their own clothes, and made their own soap.

Everyone in the household was involved in production for the household. The parents regarded building capital for their children as one of their most important roles. The mother and daughters worked to accumulate the goods necessary for the daughters to set up their own households when they got married. The father and sons worked to accumulate land and clear it. The children, in turn, were expected to help their parents during their old age.

For the Ballard family, economic success (indeed, economic survival) depended upon their collective ability to do a wide variety of things. The growth of the American economy described in chapter 3 fundamentally changed the way households pursue economic success.

Productivity increases and rising incomes made it possible for many parents to earn enough income to provide the family with the necessities of life. Children were sent to school instead of to work. The shift from work to school is shown in Figure 6.3. About 50 of every 100 children age five to nineteen went to school at the turn of the twentieth century. By 1970, almost 90 of every 100 school-aged children went to school.

When households have opportunities to invest in human capital through education, it reinforces long-run growth. Education promotes both the development of new useful knowledge, and education also makes it possible for people to use knowledge that is developed by others.

The improvements in useful knowledge included increases in knowledge about the spread of diseases and the importance of sanitation. Particularly around the turn of the twentieth century, improvements in sanitation and sewage disposal led to dramatic reductions in the incidence of communicable diseases. Increases in income made it possible to finance the sanitation

FIGURE 6.3
School Enrollment per 100 Children Aged 5–19, 1850–1970

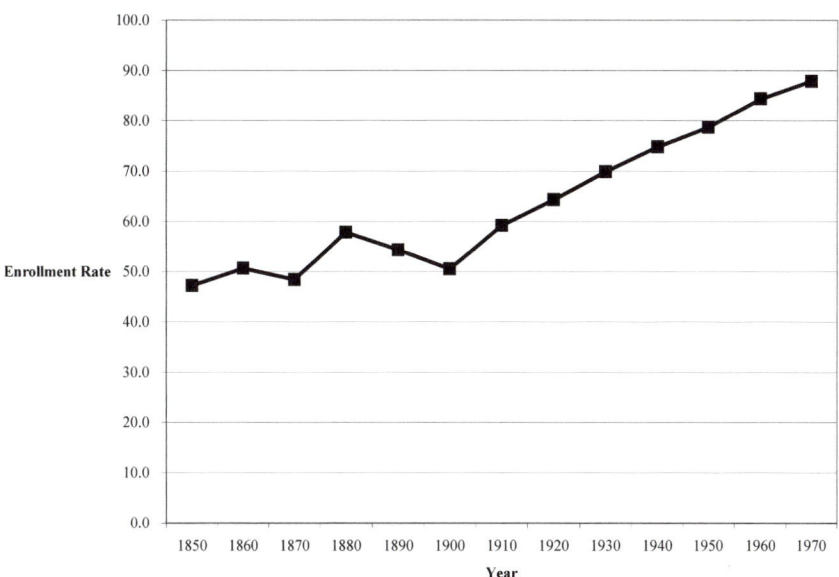

Source: U.S. Census Bureau, *Historical Statistics of the United States on CD-ROM, Colonial Times To 1970 Bicentennial Edition*; Series H 433–441, School Enrollment Rates Per 100 Population, by Race and Sex, 1850–1970.

projects. Improvements in sanitation together with improvements in medicine improved children's odds of survival. In the late nineteenth century, more than 140 out of every 1,000 children died before their first birthday; by the mid-1950s fewer than 30 of every 1,000 children died before their first birthday.

As death rates fell, it was no longer necessary for households to have a large number of children in order to ensure that some survived. At the same time, the role that children played as a form of old age insurance became less important. The development of financial markets made it possible for households to save current income for use later in the life cycle. The creation of Social Security in the 1930s further lessened the need for children to ensure consumption in old age. Figure 6.4 shows the downward trend in birth rates from 1909 to 2002. Households today are about half as large as they were at the turn of the century. The fall in the birth rate, consequent to a fall in the death rate, is a demographic pattern common to developed economies. The pattern is called the demographic transition.

Note the jump in the birth rate in the years after World War II, shown in Figure 6.4. This is the "baby boom." During the Depression and

FIGURE 6.4
Births per 1,000 People, 1909–2001

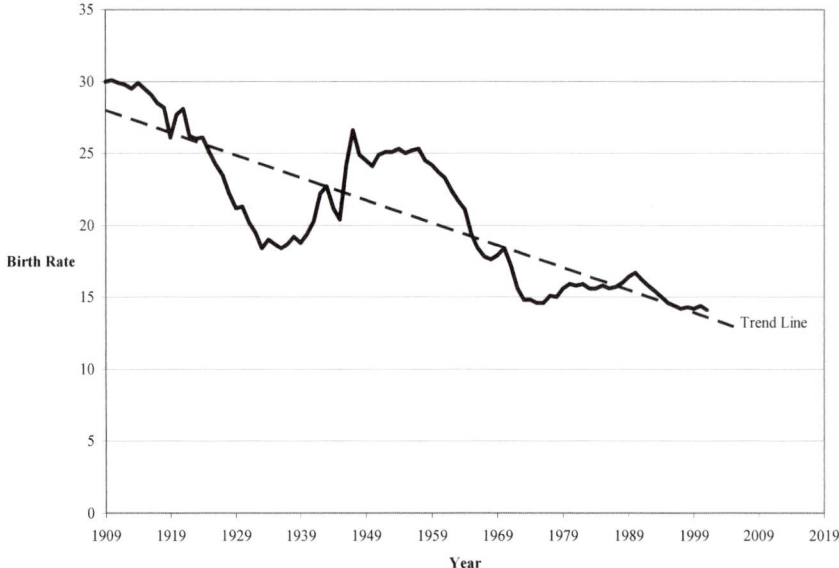

Source: Mini Historical Statistics, No. HS-13. Live Births, Deaths, Infant Deaths, and Maternal Deaths: 1900 to 2001, http://www.census.gov/statab/www/minihs.html.

World War II, people put off starting families. After World War II, many people were both willing and financially able to start families. The baby boom was a temporary break in the downward trend of the birth rate.

Finally, as markets and the division of labor expanded, it became possible to purchase many of the goods and services that had previously been produced at home, such as food, clothing, and child care.

With lower birth rates and the ability to purchase more and more goods through markets, including child care, the percentage of working-age women in the labor force, called the participation rate, increased from 36 percent in 1955 to 60 percent in 2000. The participation rate for single women rose from 61 percent to 68 percent, but the participation rate for married women rose from 29 percent to 61 percent.

Growth increased the economic independence of women by increasing their ability to earn an income and to purchase services in the marketplace. Economic independence expanded the scope of women's other choices. Women in the modern economy are able to choose between single parenting and parenting with an income-earning spouse. As late as the 1940s, 90 percent of households were classified as family households, and three-fourths of all households included a married couple. By the 1990s, only

70 percent of households were family households and just over half of households included a married couple.

HOUSEHOLD PRODUCTION

While production of goods and services within the household is in many ways less central to the economy than it was in the past, it remains important. Just like restaurants, households buy food and turn it into meals, and just like day care centers, households use labor to produce child care. The difference between households and businesses is that households consume their own production rather than selling it in markets. Consequently, household production is not counted anywhere in the national income and product accounts.

If a person ceases to purchase day care for his child and instead takes care of the child at home, GDP is reduced. The purchased day care was a service sold in the market, and home care of the child is not. This shortcoming in the measurement of economic activity is one of the many problems with comparing GDP in a modern economy like the United States with GDP in a less developed economy, and with comparing GDP today with GDP in the past.

Seven

Government and the National Economy

There are many different governments in the United States. There is one federal government; there are also 50 state governments, 3,004 county governments, 19,372 municipal governments, and 16,629 town governments. Taken together, the state and local governments are larger than the federal government in terms of expenditures and employment. In 2003 there were 2,690,000 civilian employees of the federal government and 18,349,000 state and local workers; the federal government spent $752 billion on goods and services while state and local governments spent $1.3 trillion.

What all of the levels of government have in common is that they can make rules and then legally use force to coerce people to follow the rules. The government can legally take a person's money, property, freedom, or even his life to coerce him to follow the rules.

Governments use their powers of rule-making and coercion to influence the economy. Traditionally, economists emphasized that government may be able to improve economic outcomes in situations in which markets do not work well. These situations are called market failures. Market failures can be grouped into three categories: public goods, externalities, and monopolies.

While many government actions relate to market failures, there are government actions that are not easily explained as attempts to solve the problems of market failure. For example, the government promotes or inhibits long-term growth by establishing the basic institutions under which households and businesses operate. Governments try to stabilize the economy. And governments attempt to redistribute wealth and income.

GOVERNMENT AND MARKET FAILURES

To understand market failure, we must first be clear about what it means to say that markets "work well." The first sense in which markets work well is that they maximize the benefits of trade. In markets, a person engages in a trade only when it makes him better off than he would be without the trade (see chapter 1). Every person who can benefit as either a buyer or seller is free to trade in the market; no one who feels he cannot benefit is required to trade. Because markets exhaust the possibilities for trades that benefit both buyers and sellers, markets maximize the benefits to society from trading.

Markets also encourage businesses to produce what consumers want, to produce it at the lowest possible cost, and to come up with new and better ways to do things (see chapter 5). The development of new and better ways to do things leads to increased productivity and higher standards of living.

Two conditions must be met to ensure that these benefits actually materialize. First, people have to receive all of the benefits and incur all of the costs of their choices. Second, markets have to be competitive. When these conditions are not met, we cannot be as confident about the benefits of market outcomes. Such situations are called market failures.

EXTERNALITIES

When a person does not incur all of the costs or receive all of the benefits of his choices, there are externalities. Externalities are costs or benefits that spill over onto bystanders. A negative externality is a cost that spills over on to bystanders; a positive externality is a benefit that spills over onto bystanders.

For example, an externality can arise when a person chooses to smoke a cigar in a public place. The person's choice almost certainly affects bystanders. It may be that the person next to the smoker enjoys the smell of cigar smoke and, therefore, benefits from the choice. That person experiences a positive externality. Alternatively, it may be that the person next to the smoker does not enjoy the smell of cigar smoke and, therefore, suffers a cost as the result of the choice. That person experiences a negative externality.

Common examples of situations that give rise to negative externalities are loud stereos, litter, congestion on public roadways, and water and air pollution. Examples of situations that give rise to positive externalities include flu shots, education, and public transportation. Externalities can be created either in the act of producing something, like pollution from a factory, or in the process of consuming something, like cigarettes.

Externalities arise when property rights are not clearly assigned and enforced. Property rights are legal rights to use something, receive income from it, and dispose of it. Often the failure to assign and enforce property rights arises from characteristics of the good.

Goods that are private property have two characteristics. They are rival and they are excludable. Rival means that one person's consumption of the good diminishes the benefit that someone else gets from consuming it. The benefit that a person gains from a house or apartment is diminished if a stranger moves in. The benefit that a person gains from a cup of coffee is diminished if someone else drinks it. Excludable means that it is relatively easy to define and enforce a person's property right. It is relatively easy to define the property that is your home and to keep other people from using it. It is easy to define and enforce your rights over your cup of coffee.

Negative externalities arise in situations in which something that people value is rival but not excludable. One person's consumption diminishes the benefit that others receive, but it is difficult to keep people from using it. The air is rival and not excludable. It is difficult to define and enforce rights to the air in a person's immediate vicinity. The cigar smoker is using air around another person in a way that makes the other person worse off. There are a variety of things we can do to keep people from using our home: We can put up a fence; we can lock our door; we can buy a dog. But such options are not available to keep other people from putting smoke or perfume or noise into your airspace. If we could assign and enforce property rights to the air around us the way we assign property rights to land, there would be no externality. Someone who wanted to use the air around you would have to pay.

Because people are able to use a valuable good without paying for it, they tend to do things that create negative externalities too much. If people had to take into consideration all of the costs of their actions, they would smoke fewer cigars, drive less, and fish less. Drivers only consider the cost to themselves of driving a car. They do not consider the costs they impose on others by adding to pollution and traffic congestion. A fisherman considers only the cost of operating his fishing boat. He does not consider the cost to other fishermen he causes by contributing to depletion of the fish stock.

Public policies for correcting negative externalities aim to either restrict the activity or make people bear the full cost of their choices. Government sometimes restricts choices directly by prohibiting people from creating too much of a negative externality. For instance, the government response to the decline of cod fisheries in New England has been to reduce the number of days the fishermen can fish for cod. Similarly, the government may prohibit firms from putting more than a certain amount of pollutants into the air, or prohibit them from putting a harmful substance into their product. For example, paint and gas can no longer contain lead. Government may also try to make people bear the full cost of a choice through fees or taxes. For example, governments tax pollutants that are emitted from factories, and they put so-called "sin taxes" on liquor and cigarettes.

In some situations it may be possible for the government to assign property rights to eliminate the externality. One example of this is pollution permits. The government can create property rights over the air and require anyone who wishes to put pollution into the air to purchase a pollution permit. By limiting the number of permits, the government can control the overall level of pollution.

Economists generally prefer approaches that assign property rights because these approaches reduce pollution in the most efficient way. Firms that have the greatest difficulty reducing their emissions buy permits, while firms that can reduce their emissions with little effort do that instead of buying permits. In addition, environmental groups that wish to see even less pollution than the government allows can buy the permits to take them off the market.

Positive externalities arise in situations in which a good is (at least to some degree) neither excludable nor rival. For example, when we get a flu shot, it creates a benefit for all the people that are less likely to get the flu from us. We cannot exclude them from this benefit, nor does their benefit diminish our own benefit from the flu shot.

A good does not have to be completely nonrival and nonexcludable to create a positive externality. It is possible to exclude people from education: A private school excludes those who do not pay tuition. However, the directors of the private school cannot exclude everyone from the benefits that come from having better-educated people in their society.

Public Goods

Goods that are completely nonrival and nonexcludable are called public goods. National defense is a public good. If we create an army that keeps foreign governments from invading, we cannot exclude some people within our borders from the benefit of security. In addition, one person's benefit from security in no way diminishes another person's benefit. Although public goods are often discussed as a problem separate from externalities, a public good is really just an extreme version of a positive externality.

Positive externalities create a "problem" because when people make choices, they consider only the benefit to themselves rather than the total benefit of their choices to society. Therefore, people tend to do less of the things that create a positive externality than would be best for society.

We say that public goods have a "free rider problem." Because a good is nonexcludable, people are able to get a free ride when someone else purchases the good. But if everyone waits to get a free ride off of someone else, then the good is not purchased at all. Government responds to positive externalities by using subsidies to encourage people to purchase more of the good, or by taxing everyone to pay for the purchase of the good by the government.

The government usually gets involved when the costs or benefits of the externality is substantial. Because we live together in society, we affect each other in many small ways all the time. It would be impossibly expensive for the government to regulate all possible externalities. For example, if you do not like someone's perfume, it's a negative externality for you, but we do not expect the government to regulate perfume. If you dislike the color of your neighbor's house, it is a negative externality for you, but we do not expect the government to regulate paint colors.

Monopoly

In addition to externalities, market failures arise from monopoly. Monopoly is the lack of competition in a market. Without competition, a firm may be able to earn high profits by restricting the supply and driving up the price, reducing the benefits to consumers. The section on competition and pricing in chapter 5 explains that two things are necessary for a firm to have monopoly or market power. First, there must be no close substitutes for the product of the firm. If there are close substitutes, people switch to them when a firm raises its price. Second, the firm must have a means of preventing new firms from entering the market; there must be a barrier to entry. If there is no barrier to entry, then the firm's profits attract entrepreneurs into the market. The entry of competitors drives down the firm's prices and profits.

There are three approaches to government intervention regarding monopolies. The first approach is to promote competition. The second approach is to allow a monopoly to exist, but to regulate it. The last approach is to do nothing in the belief that government involvement is likely to make the situation worse, not better.

Promoting Competition with Antitrust Law

The first approach to monopoly, promoting competition, is the goal of antitrust law. The role of the government in promoting competition is often dated to the passage of the Sherman Antitrust Act in 1890. This is a little misleading. By 1890, many states already had antimonopoly laws. Moreover, restrictions against anticompetitive actions can be traced to the common law. The Sherman Act did, however, signal the entry of the federal government into the regulation of competition. Section 1 of the Sherman

Act declares that any "contract, combination, or conspiracy in restraint of trade" is illegal. Section 2 declares that anyone who "monopolizes or attempts to monopolize" a market is in violation of the law.

The application of antitrust law is complicated by the fact that monopoly power is a matter of degree. There are few, if any, goods that have absolutely no substitutes and few, if any, markets in which there are absolute barriers to entry.

Because it is not easy to say when a firm is a monopoly and when it is not, the Supreme Court plays an important role in antitrust regulation by interpreting the meaning of the law. In 1911 the court introduced the rule of reason in a decision that broke up Standard Oil Company into a number of smaller firms. According to the rule of reason, mere size is not, in itself, a violation of the law. If a firm obtains its large share of a market by producing a better product at a lower price than its competitors, the firm is not in violation of the law. However, if a firm competes unfairly to drive other firms from the market, it is in violation.

The Sherman Act was supplemented by the Clayton Act (1914), the Federal Trade Commission Act (1914), and the Robinson-Patman Act (1936). These acts clarify the actions that are unreasonable and violations of the law, and the Federal Trade Commission Act empowers the FTC to enforce fair trade practices. Examples of illegal actions include mergers that reduce competition and contracts that restrict a buyer from dealing with other sellers.

An antitrust case can be brought to court by private citizens or by the Justice Department. The FTC brings cases before its own administrative law judges. Antitrust cases can result in cease-and-desist orders or injunctions that prohibit the firm from continuing the actions that have been determined to be in violation of the law. Cases can also result in a consent decree. In a consent decree, the firm does not admit to any wrongdoing, but does agree to change its behavior. A firm found guilty of violating antitrust law can be held liable for three times the damage that it caused.

Promoting competition makes economic sense when firms conspire to prevent competition. In such a case, consumers pay higher prices and there is no benefit to society from the monopoly. Some monopolies, however, can benefit society in the form of having lower costs of production. In the case of a "natural" monopoly, society is better off with a monopoly that is regulated by the government, and it is not desirable to promote competition.

Natural Monopoly and Regulation

A natural monopoly exists when one firm can meet the demands of the market more cheaply than two or more firms. Natural monopolies tend to exist in markets where there are high start-up costs, but a low cost of providing the good to an additional customer. For instance, the start-up cost for a business to provide water to houses is high. In addition to the water purification plant, there is the cost of running pipes to all of houses in the market. But the water company is able to spread the start-up costs over many customers, and the cost of running pipes to one more house is small. Creating competition by duplicating the water system would not be beneficial. Each company would have the same start-up costs, but a smaller number of customers to spread the cost over. The government response to natural monopolies is usually to regulate the rates they charge. Generally, these companies are regulated at the state or local level.

Laissez-faire *Approach To Monopoly*

The last approach to dealing with monopoly is a laissez-faire, or hands-off, approach. Advocates of a hands-off approach have two arguments. First, they argue that monopoly profits drive innovation. A firm innovates in order to be the first and only firm in a market. The United States recognizes and encourages such monopoly through innovation by awarding patents. Patents give people property rights over their innovation in exchange for making the knowledge public. Second, advocates of doing nothing about monopolies argue that substantial barriers to entry rarely exist. Even patents, which are intended to create a barrier to entry, cannot prevent firms from creating substitutes that are sufficiently different that they do not violate the patent.

Advocates of doing nothing point to a 1969 Justice Department suit against IBM, alleging that IBM attempted to monopolize the market for general-purpose computers. The case dragged on for years, at great expense to both IBM and the government. Finally in 1982, the Justice Department dropped the case after it concluded that even if IBM had a monopoly in 1969, it no longer did.

Market Failure Versus Government Failure

Although government regulation may improve market outcomes when a market failure exists, we should take care not to expect government to provide a perfect solution. Economist Howard Demsetz cautioned people not to fall into the Nirvana fallacy. The Nirvana fallacy refers to the concept of a state of perfection in Eastern religions. Demsetz warned that we should not compare imperfect markets with a hypothetical perfect government. Because governments are run by imperfect people, government regulation is unlikely to be perfect.

GOVERNMENT BUDGETS

To produce public goods and services, the government must claim some of society's resources. The government must impose taxes of one sort or another. The most widely used taxes in the United States are payroll taxes, income taxes, property taxes, and sales taxes. The government also imposes tariffs on some imported goods. Taxes on exports are prohibited by the Constitution.

Figure 7.1 shows the relative importance of the different sources of revenue for the federal government in 2003. By far the largest are individual income taxes and social insurance contributions. Excise taxes are taxes on specific goods. The excise tax that produces the most revenue for the federal government is the tax on alcohol.

FIGURE 7.1
Distribution of Federal Spending, 2003

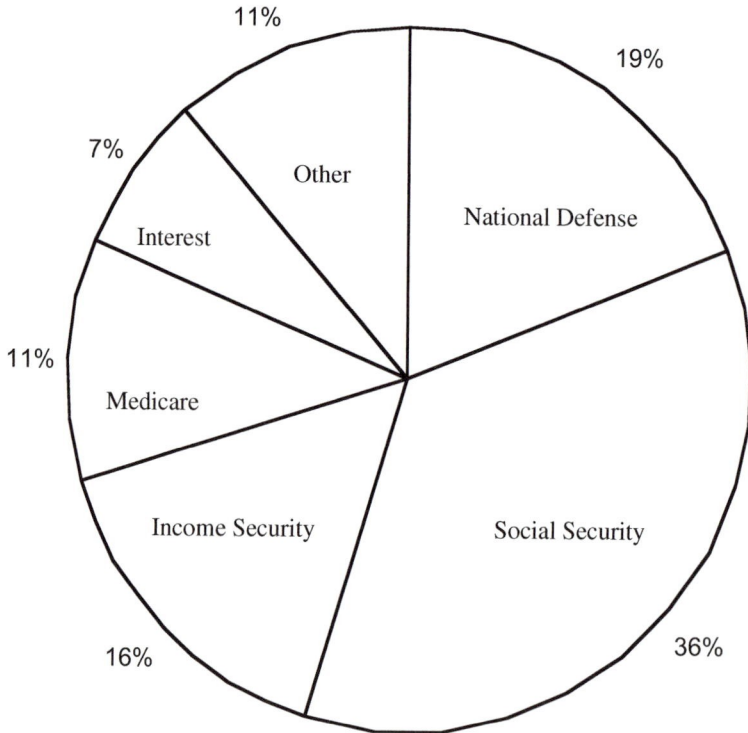

Source: Statistical Abstract of the United States, 2005; Table No. 462, Federal Budget Outlays—Defense, Human, and Physical Resources, and Net Interest Payments: 1990–2004.

Taxes can be progressive or regressive. A tax is progressive if the percentage of her income that a person pays increases as her income increases. A tax is regressive if the percentage of her income that a person pays decreases as her income increases. Despite the obvious connotation of the names, there is nothing inherently good in a progressive tax or inherently bad in a regressive tax.

The individual income tax in the United States is an example of a progressive tax. As a person's income rises, he moves into a "higher tax bracket," which means a larger percentage of income is paid in taxes. The thresholds between tax brackets depend on a variety of things: whether a person is single or married, whether he has dependents, and how many dependents he has. Table 7.1 shows the tax schedule for a single person in 2005. An individual is taxed 10 percent on the first $7,300 of income, and 15 percent on the next $22,400.

Figure 7.2 shows the relative importance of different categories of spending in the federal budget. The budget includes both mandatory and discretionary spending. Mandatory spending is spending that the government is bound by law to do, such as Social Security, Medicare, Medicaid, retirement for federal civil servants, and interest on the national debt. Currently, mandatory payments make up over 60 percent of the budget. Defense expenditures make up about 20 percent of the total outlays.

The budget of the federal government covers a fiscal year that runs from October 1 to September 30. When spending exceeds revenue over the course of a fiscal year, the government runs a budget deficit. The government has to borrow to cover the deficit. The federal government borrows by issuing Treasury bills, notes, and bonds. Bills are loans that are repaid within a year. Notes are repaid in ten years or less, and bonds have a maturity of ten years

TABLE 7.1
Tax Schedule for a Single Filer, 2005

If taxable income is over—	But not over—	The tax is:
$0	$7,300	10% of the amount over $0
$7,300	$29,700	$730 plus 15% of the amount over 7,300
$29,700	$71,950	$4,090.00 plus 25% of the amount over 29,700
$71,950	$150,150	$14,652.50 plus 28% of the amount over 71,950
$150,150	$326,450	$36,548.50 plus 33% of the amount over 150,150
$326,450	no limit	$94,727.50 plus 35% of the amount over 326,450

Source: U.S. Internal Revenue Service, 2005 Tax Rate Schedules, http://www.irs.gov/formspubs/article/0,,id=133517,00.html.

FIGURE 7.2
Distribution of Federal Government Revenues, 2003

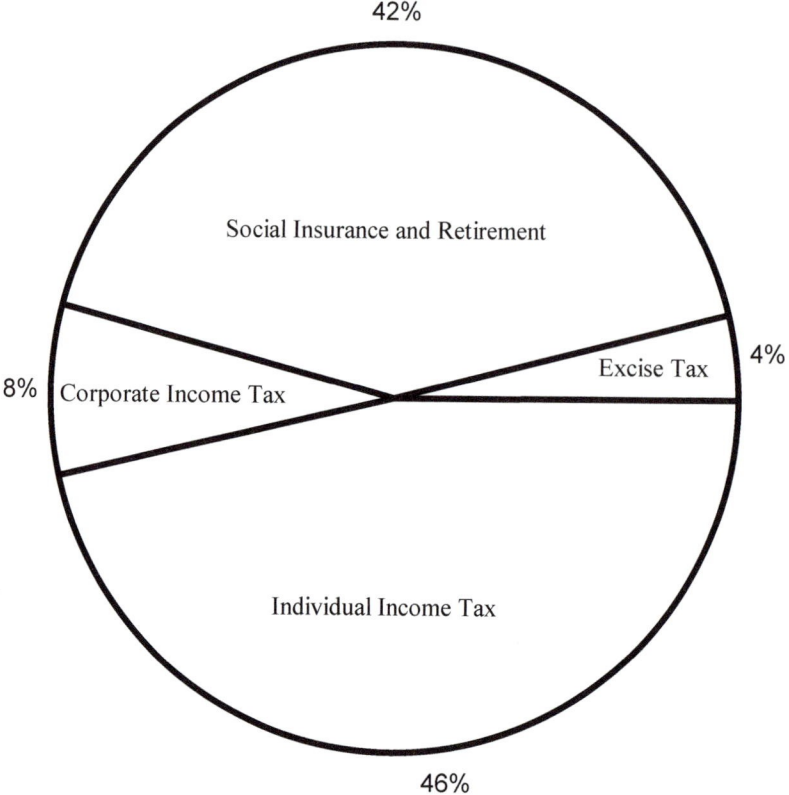

Source: U.S. Census Bureau, *Statistical Abstract of the United States, 2005.* Table No. 467 Federal Receipts by Source: 1990–2004.

or more. The national debt is the sum of all the past deficits, plus interest paid, minus the borrowing that has been paid back.

Like the federal government, state and local governments create budgets for their revenues and spending. In 2001, almost one-third of state and local spending went to education. The rest of state and local spending went to welfare, highways, fire and police protection, health, hospitals, prisons, sanitation, utilities, parks and recreation, and miscellaneous other expenditures.

Approximately 17 percent of state and local government revenue came from transfers from the federal government. Other state and local government revenue came from individual income taxes, sales taxes, property taxes, and corporate taxes. The mix of types of taxes used varies from one state to another.

The Federal Deficit

The federal government has run a budget deficit in all but four of the last thirty-five years. In 2002, 2003, and 2004 the deficit was equal to about 3 percent of GDP. As a percentage of GDP, current deficits pale in comparison with those of World War II. In 1943 the federal deficit was equal to 30 percent of GDP. Running a deficit requires the government to borrow to make up the difference. The effects of the deficit on the economy arise from this borrowing. The first concern is crowding out. By entering the market for loanable funds, the government drives up the interest rate and reduces private investment. The second concern is that, by raising interest rates in the United States, deficits encourage foreign lenders to put their money in the United States. Other things being equal, if U.S. bonds pay higher interest rates, people are more likely to buy them. Foreigners lending to the United States help offset the crowding-out problem, but foreigners have to first buy U.S. dollars before they can buy U.S. bonds. The increased demand for dollars makes the price of dollars (the exchange rate) rise. As the dollar becomes more expensive for foreigners, it also becomes more expensive for them to purchase U.S. goods. In sum, an increasing federal deficit can also cause an increasing trade deficit. This connection has led to talk of the "twin deficits" that arose in the 1980s as budget deficits began to escalate. In the final analysis, whether or not a trade deficit is a good thing or a bad thing depends on what the borrowing is for. Few people dispute the value of military spending during World War II. On the other hand, to the extent that current borrowing is primarily to support current consumption, the benefits are less obvious.

THE ECONOMIC IMPACT OF TAXES

All taxes alter the choices that people make by altering the costs and benefits of choices. Two features of taxes are important for understanding how they influence incentives and choices.

1. Taxes drive a wedge between what buyers pay and what sellers receive from exchange. Taxes drive up costs for buyers and drive down benefits for sellers.
2. The person who really pays a tax is not necessarily the same person who is assessed for the tax by the government.

To see how taxes affect exchange and market outcomes, consider the example of a tax on cigarettes illustrated in Figure 7.3. The original market equilibrium, where supply and demand intersect, is at a price of $5 and a quantity of 500 packs of cigarettes. Suppose sellers are assessed a tax of $2 on each pack of cigarettes sold. Initially we may assume that sellers will try to pass the cost of the tax on to buyers. Unfortunately for sellers, the number of packs of cigarettes that people are willing and able to buy decreases as the price goes up. Smokers are not willing to purchase 500 packs at $7.00 a pack; they want fewer at the higher price. To prevent the loss of too many customers, sellers take some of the cost of the tax on themselves. Figure 7.3 shows that in this case buyers end up paying $6 per pack (instead of the original $5); sellers give $2 per pack in taxes to the government, so sellers are left with $4 dollars per pack (instead of the original $5) after the tax. A wedge is driven between what the buyers pay and what the sellers get to keep. The wedge is equal to the size of the tax. Note also that only 400 packs of cigarettes are sold after the tax is assessed (instead of the original 500).

Although the tax assessment of $2 per pack was made on the sellers, the sellers did not end up with $2 less per pack, and the buyers did not end up paying $2 more per pack. The burden of the tax was split between buyers and sellers; each paid one-half of the tax.

FIGURE 7.3
Impact of a $2.00-a-Pack Cigarette Tax

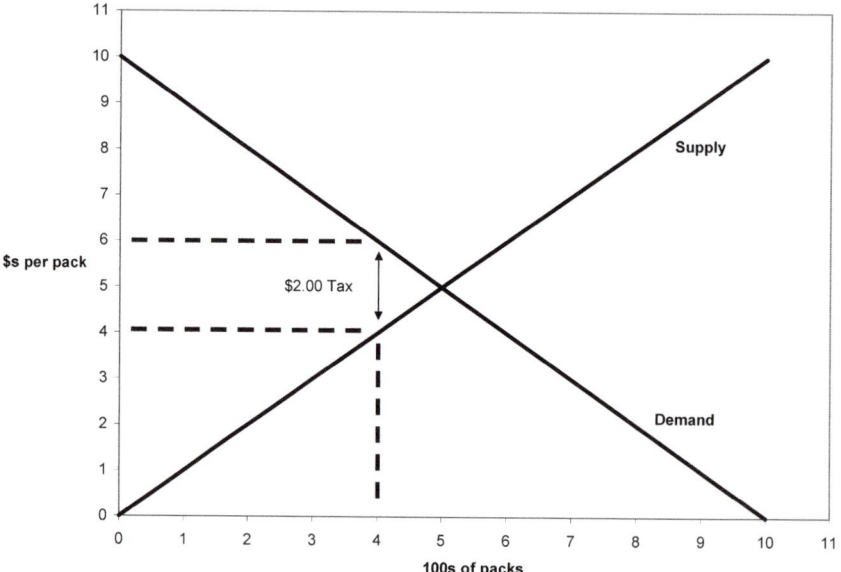

The burden of the tax is not always split equally between buyers and sellers. The group that can more easily avoid the tax pays less of it. For buyers, being able to avoid the tax means that they have available to them substitutes that are not taxed, or at least not taxed as heavily. Consider what happens if a city puts a tax on cigarettes, but the county next to the city has no tax on cigarettes. Sellers in the city cannot pass much of the tax on to buyers because then the buyers simply go to the next county to purchase their cigarettes. Sellers in the city end up paying most of the cost of the tax.

GOVERNMENT AND ECONOMIC GROWTH

Chapter 3 explained how well-functioning markets provide strong incentives to make choices that promote growth. Consequently, the most important step that a government can take to promote economic growth is to support well-functioning markets. As discussed above, markets function well if they have institutions that protect property rights.

A property right is the right to control the use of a resource and the income from it. Without control of the income generated by use of their resources, people do not choose to use their resources in the ways that generate economic growth. For example, for a person to choose to use her resources to open a factory, she must feel certain that the factory itself and the profits from the factory are protected. Without this assurance, without secure property rights, she is likely to use her resources differently. Similarly, when a person spends time inventing a new technology, he gives up time spent fishing. Without the assurance of a patent, so that he can be sure of profiting from his invention, the person is more likely to go fishing.

Property has to be protected from three threats. First, it has to be protected from foreigners. National defense protects people and their property from threats from abroad. Second, it has to be protected from other people within the society. Police protect people and their property from other citizens. Finally, property has to be protected from the government itself. In some ways this can be the most tricky since the government has a legal right to use force. Protection from arbitrary confiscation by the government requires a system of checks and balances as well as social norms that discourage government corruption.

Governments can also promote well-functioning markets and economic growth by establishing institutions that lower transaction costs. Institutions lower transaction costs by helping people make credible commitments. A commitment is an obligation to do something: to repay a debt, to perform a service, to provide a good. A credible commitment is one that is believable.

Public works and infrastructure development projects—your tax dollars at work. Getty Images: Arthur S. Aubry.

Trades that involve complicated goods or that take place over time are unlikely to occur if people are not expected to fulfill their obligations.

For a commitment to be believable it has to be clear that it will be in a person's best interest to live up to his obligation. Contract law encourages a person to fulfill his contractual obligations by giving him the choice of fulfilling his contract or paying for the damage that he caused the other party to the contract. Contract law makes commitments more credible by imposing a cost on people for not fulfilling their obligations. The law and courts also facilitate exchange by filling the gaps in contracts. It is impossible to write a contract that accounts for every possible contingency. The law settles disputes when something arises that is not spelled out in the contract.

Because markets do not do a good job providing public goods and goods with positive externalities, government can promote growth by investing directly in the types of physical capital that are not rival or excludable. Roads, bridges, ports, water and power, and the Internet are all goods that have been produced by the government in the past in order to promote growth in the future. Governments can also promote growth by producing things that have positive externalities. For example, the government may directly support the development of new knowledge (such as scientific research at NASA and the NIH), and the government may provide the education (at public schools, community colleges, and universities) necessary for its citizens to use that knowledge.

After secure property rights, laws that lower transaction costs, and the provision of public goods, government can also try to shape tax law to encourage work, saving, and investment. The tax system that encourages work, saving, and investment is a system based on taxes on consumption (sales taxes), not taxes on income. Taxes on income discourage work, savings, and investment.

STABILIZING THE ECONOMY

The Employment Act of 1946 formally required the federal government to take steps to promote "maximum employment, production, and purchasing power." The Humphrey-Hawkins Act of 1978 reaffirmed the federal government's responsibility for promoting economic stability.

It is easy to agree that stable prices, maximum growth, and full employment are good things. However, as we saw in chapter 4, economists are split between Keynesian and Classical views on the causes of business cycle movements and how to respond to them. Policy-makers also disagree about the appropriate use of fiscal and monetary policy. Fiscal policy refers to policy on taxing and spending. Monetary policy refers to actions the Federal Reserve takes that influence the money supply and interest rates. Decisions about fiscal policy are made by the president and Congress. The president submits a suggested budget to Congress, and Congress has the ultimate say about both taxes and spending. Decisions about monetary policy are made by the Federal Open Market Committee of the Federal Reserve.

Fiscal Policy, Crowding Out, and Automatic Stabilizers

Keynesian economists and policy-makers are most likely to support active fiscal policies to stabilize the economy. They believe that the government can manage aggregate demand through either fiscal or monetary policy. The government can counteract a recession by cutting taxes or increasing government expenditures. The Federal Reserve can respond to a recession by increasing the money supply and lowering interest rates. Government can respond to inflation by decreasing aggregate demand: increasing taxes, lowering spending, reducing the money supply, and raising interest rates.

Classical economists believe that fiscal policy does not affect aggregate demand. They believe the primary effect of changes in government spending is on the distribution of goods and services, not on the total amount produced. As discussed in chapter 4, Classical economists believe that a market economy always tends to move toward its potential output. Potential output depends on available resources and productivity and is independent of today's fiscal policy. If government increases spending while total output remains unchanged, then the amount of output available for private households and firms must decrease. The amount of output households and firms get decreases because the government has to pay for its increased spending by either increasing taxes or increasing borrowing. If government increases taxes, households have less income to spend. If government borrows more, there is less savings available for businesses to use for private investment. When private investment falls as a result of increasing government spending, we say that government spending "crowds out" private investment.

In addition to the problem of crowding out, classical economists note that it is not quick or easy to change fiscal policy. A spending bill has to go through congressional committees before it can come up for a vote. The bill has to be passed by both the House and Senate. The president must sign the bill into law. All this takes time. It is likely to be nearly a year before a change in fiscal policy can be put in place, by which time market forces may have already moved the economy back toward its potential. The increase in spending may actually happen as the economy is on an upswing; fiscal policy may actually cause economic instability rather than fix it.

Keynesians recognize the problem of crowding out, but they argue that there can be crowding in as well. Businesses that postponed investment because they were pessimistic about the state of the economy may decide to start investing as a result of the increase in demand generated by government spending. Keynesians argue that the problem of delay in enacting fiscal policy can be overcome by enacting laws that put automatic stabilizers in place. Automatic stabilizers are programs that are part of mandatory government spending and that change automatically as the economy expands or contracts. An example is unemployment benefits. If the economy is in recession and unemployment increases, more people file for unemployment benefits, so government spending automatically increases. Progressive income taxes are also an automatic stabilizer, because tax revenue automatically increases as income increases and people move into higher tax brackets, and automatically decreases as incomes fall and people move into lower tax brackets.

The Federal Reserve and Monetary Policy

The Federal Reserve System, established in 1913, is the central bank of the United States. The Federal Reserve has three duties: It regulates other banks, it acts as a banker for the federal government, and it conducts monetary policy.

The Federal Reserve System, as the name suggests, is not a single entity. The Federal Reserve System is composed of twelve regional Federal Reserve banks, a board of governors, and the Federal Open Market Committee (FOMC). Federal Reserve Banks are located in the following cities: Boston, New York, Philadelphia, Cleveland, Richmond, Atlanta, Chicago, St. Louis, Minneapolis, Kansas City, Dallas, and San Francisco. The regional banks are owned by private member banks in the region, and the president of each regional bank is appointed by the board of directors of the regional bank. The board of governors has seven members, appointed by the president and confirmed by Congress for fourteen-year terms. The president also appoints one of the governors as chairman for a four-year term. The FOMC consists of all the governors, the president of the Federal Reserve Bank of New York, and four other presidents of regional banks who serve on a rotating basis.

The Federal Reserve System is a complicated hybrid; it is a mix of public and private entity spread all over the country. The intention of the writers of the Federal Reserve Act was to spread out the power of the central bank. The Federal Reserve is an independent central bank. Monetary policy is not directly under the control of elected officials the way that fiscal policy is. The president cannot use monetary policy for political purposes. The president and Congress cannot insist that the Federal Reserve finance government borrowing by printing new money, a practice called "monetizing the debt." In countries where the central bank is not independent, monetizing the debt can easily lead to rapid inflation.

While the Federal Reserve is independent, it was created by Congress and is subject to federal regulation. The Humphrey-Hawkins Act requires the chairman to report to Congress on a regular basis.

The Federal Reserve influences aggregate demand through changes in interest rates. The Federal Reserve influences interest rates by changing the supply of money. Recall from chapter 1 that the money supply is made up of coins, currency, travelers checks, and checkable deposits. The interest rate is the price of money. That is, the interest rate is what we pay to use someone else's money. The market for money works the same way other markets do: A larger supply of money is associated with a lower price of money. Increasing the supply of money lowers the interest rate; decreasing the money supply increases the interest rate. Therefore, if the Federal Reserve thinks the economy is operating below its potential, it tries to lower interest rates, which encourages borrowing for investment by firms and borrowing for spending by households. If the Federal Reserve fears that the economy is being pushed beyond its potential and that inflation is accelerating, it tries to raise interest rates, discouraging borrowing, investment, and spending.

The key to understanding monetary policy in the United States is to know that the Federal Reserve does not control the interest rate or money supply directly, but instead initiates changes in the money supply by altering the amount of money that banks have available to loan out. The process of loan-making leads to a change in the money supply.

When customers make deposits at a bank, the bank sets aside part of the deposits as reserves. Banks hold reserves to meet the needs of customers for withdrawals, but it is unlikely that customers will withdraw all of their deposits at the same time. A bank makes its profit by loaning out the deposits that it does not keep as reserves. Because reserves are only a fraction of deposits, we say that banks operate on a fractional reserve system. Reserves may be held as cash in the bank's vault or as deposits at the Federal Reserve. Banks are required to keep a certain percentage of deposits in reserve, but often keep more than required reserves. Reserves over and above the re-quired amount are called excess reserves. Excess reserves minus any reserves that have been borrowed from another bank are called free reserves.

If a bank experiences an increase in its free reserves, it can loan this money out. The loan sets off a chain of events that increases the money supply. Suppose a bank experiences an increase in its free reserves of $10,000, which it loans out to Mr. White. Mr. White uses his loan to make a purchase at Ms. Green's store. Ms. Green deposits the $10,000 in her bank. Ms. Green's bank keeps $1,000 of her deposit as reserves and loans out $9,000 to Mr. Pink. Mr. Pink spends the $9,000 at Mrs. Brown's store. Mrs. Brown then deposits the $9,000 in her bank. Mrs. Brown now has $9,000 more money in the bank than before. Yet Ms. Green still has her $10,000 in the bank. The amount of money in the economy has gone up, not just by $10,000, but by $19,000—and it doesn't stop there. Mrs. Brown's bank now lends out part of the $9,000 that she deposited. That money eventually ends up as deposits in another bank, and so on. The process by which an initial change in reserves increases the money supply by an amount larger than that initial change is called the "money multiplier" process.

The more banks keep in reserve, the smaller the money multiplier is. To see why, consider what would happen if banks held 100 percent of deposits in reserve. After the deposit by Ms. Green, the process would end. There would be no further loans, no more deposits. On the other hand, if banks kept no reserves, the money multiplier would be infinite. One bank would loan out $10,000, which would get deposited in another bank, which would also lend out $10,000, and it would just keep going.

To influence free reserves, the Federal Reserve has three tools: the reserve requirement, open market operations, and the discount rate. Changing the reserve requirement directly influences the amount of free reserves. If a bank has $10 million in deposits and a 10 percent reserve requirement, it must hold at least $1 million in reserves. If the Federal Reserve lowers the reserve requirement to 5 percent, the bank has to keep only $500,000 on reserve for that $10 million in deposits. It has an additional $500,000 it can lend out. Lending out the $500,000 will set in motion the money multiplier.

Open market operations also directly influence free reserves. An open market operation by the Federal Reserve is a purchase or sale of a U.S. government security. If the Federal Reserve wants to increase free reserves, it can buy a security from a bank and pay for it by crediting the bank's account at a Federal Reserve bank. The bank has free reserves that it can lend out. If the Federal Reserve wants to reduce the money supply, it can sell a security to a bank and subtract the sale price from the bank's reserves. The bank must then reduce its outstanding loans, which sets the money multiplier into reverse.

Sometimes a bank finds that it does not have enough reserves to meet the reserve requirement. The bank must borrow to make up the shortfall. The bank can borrow from the Fed or from another bank. The interest rate the bank pays when it borrows from the Federal Reserve is called the discount rate, and the process of borrowing from the Federal Reserve is called going to the discount window. If the Fed lowers the discount rate, it can lead to an increase in reserves by lowering the cost of borrowing reserves. The interest rate the bank pays when it borrows from another bank is called the federal funds rate. The Fed does not directly control the federal funds rate, but it sets a target for the federal funds rate and then uses its tools of monetary policy to achieve those targets.

The money multiplier shows how the Federal Reserve influences the supply of money. It also shows that the Federal Reserve is not the only party that influences the money supply. Decisions made by banks and by people also influence the money supply. If banks choose to hold more free reserves and not lend out the new deposits, it reduces the money multiplier effect. If people choose not to put their money into bank accounts, it also reduces the money multiplier effect.

Because of the complicated nature of the process, monetary policy affects the economy with long and variable lags. In other words, it takes months, if not years, for a change in monetary policy to have its full effect. Further, it is difficult to predict exactly how long the process may take. Because of the long and variable lags, some Classical economists argue that the Fed should follow a rule rather than actively try to manage interest rates. These economists are called "monetarists." The most well-known monetarist is the Nobel Prize winner Milton Friedman, who advocates that the Fed increase the money supply at a constant rate consistent with the long run rate of growth of real output, about 3 percent per year.

The part of the Fed that makes decisions about monetary policy is the Federal Open Market Committee. The FOMC meets regularly eight times per year. The outcome of FOMC meetings is a decision about the current target for the federal funds rate and the likely direction of future changes in the target. For instance, the outcome of the FOMC's August 9, 2005, meeting was the announcement: "The Federal Open Market Committee decided today to raise its target for the federal funds rate by 25 basis points to 3-1/2 percent." A basis point is one one-hundredth of a percentage point, so the target was increased from 3.25 to 3.5 percent.

Newspapers sometimes report a bit mistakenly that the Fed has raised or lowered interest rates. This is misleading because the only interest rate the Fed directly controls is the discount rate. In addition, the discount rate and the federal funds rate do not directly affect business and consumer borrowers. They apply only to loans from the Fed to a bank or from one bank to another. It is essential to recognize that the Fed does not simply set interest rates in the economy; they are determined by supply and demand. The Fed can use its tools to try to influence interest rates, pushing them higher or lower.

The Federal Reserve uses its ability to influence interest rates to manage aggregate demand. Discussion within FOMC meetings usually focuses on where the economy is relative to its potential output. The announcement from the August 9, 2005, meeting explained that, "With appropriate monetary policy action, the upside and downside risks to the attainment of both sustainable growth and price stability should be kept roughly equal." In plain English, the FOMC said that the objective of targeting the federal funds rate a little higher was to make sure there is enough demand to keep the economy at its potential output, but not so much demand as to cause inflation by pushing the economy beyond potential output.

This task is a difficult one. No one knows for certain what potential output is, or what the natural rate of unemployment related to potential output is. The only way to be absolutely certain where potential output is at any time is to pass it, causing inflation. Alan Greenspan has characterized monetary policy-making as a matter of balancing risks: the risk of inflation versus the risk recession.

Disagreements within the FOMC in the 1990s centered on whether or not there was a "new" economy with a higher potential output and lower natural rate of unemployment than existed before. Chairman Alan Greenspan was one of the first to argue for a new economy. As the unemployment rate fell below 6 percent and then continued to fall below 5 percent, some members of the FOMC argued that the economy had certainly reached its potential output and that interest rates needed to be increased to head off inflation. In the 1980s many economists believed that the natural rate of unemployment was probably around 6 percent. Greenspan, on the other hand, argued for a continued expansionary policy because he believed that increases in productivity would enable business to meet the growth in demand without raising prices. Although there are twelve members of the FOMC, the chairman has traditionally been able to play a leading role in determining policy, and this has been the case under Greenspan. As it turns out, he was right. The FOMC maintained low interest rates, and unemployment fell to 4 percent without inflation accelerating.

THE EVOLUTION OF STABILIZATION POLICY

The association of wartime spending with the end of the Great Depression seemed like convincing evidence in support of Keynesian economic theory to some young economists, though it was decades before Keynes's views came to influence macroeconomic policy.

President John F. Kennedy was elected in 1960, at a time when the economy was slipping into a recession. The Harvard-educated Kennedy brought with him to the White House several economic advisers who advocated a Keynesian approach to economic policy. Kennedy was able to get tax cuts passed. Growth increased and unemployment fell. Many people took the success of the Kennedy tax cuts as clear evidence in support of Keynesian demand management through fiscal policy. Less attention was paid to monetary policy, which had been somewhat discredited by Keynes.

Keynesian economists recognized that increasing demand can also increase prices so that demand management involved a trade-off between higher inflation and lower unemployment. It turns out, however, that the trade-off between inflation and unemployment was not as straightforward as first thought. Maintaining unemployment below the natural rate required not just inflation, but accelerating inflation. If expansionary policy pushed the economy past potential output, prices began to rise. As prices rise, people ask for higher wages and ultimately businesses hire less labor. Unemployment returns to the natural rate. If the government keeps pushing up demand to lower unemployment, they keep pushing up prices as well. As people begin to expect higher inflation, they no longer wait until after prices have increased to demand higher wages. They start to demand higher wages in anticipation of higher prices. Just maintaining the same level of unemployment starts to require more rapid increases in prices.

The increases in unemployment in the 1970s that took place as the economy tried to adjust back to the natural rate of unemployment led to periods of both high inflation and high unemployment. These periods were called "stagflation," a combination of stagnation and inflation. Stagflation is the worst of both macroeconomic worlds, but it gave rise to an idea about how to attain the best of both worlds.

The Reagan administration, elected in 1980, advocated "supply-side" economics. Like Keynesians, they advocated tax cuts to stimulate the economy, but unlike the Keynesians, they argued that the objective was not to stimulate demand but to stimulate supply. Supply-side advocates argued that lowering taxes creates incentives for people to work and invest more, increasing supply all over the economy and lowering inflation.

Inflation did fall during the administration of Ronald Reagan (1980–88), but most economists today attribute the fall in inflation to monetary policy. Federal Reserve chairman Paul Volcker dramatically reduced the rate of growth of the money supply and increased interest rates. Despite an increase in the unemployment rate to double digits for the first time since the Great Depression, Volcker continued to restrict the growth of the money supply. He believed that it was a necessary, if painful, step to eliminate people's expectations of future inflation. Volcker's successor, Alan Greenspan, remained committed to holding down inflation, but also showed a remarkable aptitude for knowing when to stimulate demand to head off a recession.

The success of Volcker and Greenspan led to a role reversal in the relative importance of monetary and fiscal policy. Fiscal policy was regarded as the primary tool to prevent recessions in the 1960s and 1970s, while monetary policy was in the background. By the 1990s and 2000s, monetary policy was center stage. The FOMC actively tries to manage aggregate demand, and the news media closely follows statements by the chairman. Discussions of fiscal policy are about long-run considerations. For example, the economists who helped develop and advocate President George W. Bush's program to cut taxes emphasized the long-run effects of encouraging investment much more than the short-term effects of stimulating demand or supply.

GOVERNMENT AND REDISTRIBUTION

The types of government activities that we have examined so far all involve attempts to improve the performance of markets. But even when markets are working well, people may not like the outcomes. Consequently, governments are active in redistributing income and wealth. There are two types of redistribution. First, redistribution is used to try to ensure at least some reasonable standard of living for everyone. Second, redistribution is used by politically powerful groups to increase their own incomes.

Programs to redistribute income to the less fortunate may be motivated by a sense of benevolence or by a belief that they prevent social unrest. The United States currently has a number of such welfare programs. There are programs that provide insurance: Social Security and Unemployment Insurance. There are programs that provide relief to needy families and individuals: Temporary Assistance to Needy Families, Supplemental Security Income, food stamps, and school lunches. And there are programs that provide medical care: Medicare and Medicaid. Although many of these specific programs were developed in the last seventy years, welfare programs of one sort or another date back to the colonial period and earlier.

It is sometimes suggested that there was a time without welfare programs when neighbors looked after each other, but the United States has always had government welfare programs. Historically, however, welfare operated on a local level rather than at the federal level. Although the details varied from place to place, these programs typically had two components: to ensure that those who were able to work did, and to ensure that those who could not work were taken care of. In many places people dependent on welfare were housed together. When people refer to "ending up in the poorhouse," it is a reference to this earlier form of welfare.

The second type of redistribution involves using the political process to shift income from one group to another. Politically influential groups are able to gain legislation that redistributes income to them. These groups gain their influence by providing resources (monetary contributions, endorsements, or other campaign support) to politicians.

The economist Mancur Olson suggested that politicians tend to enact policies that have concentrated benefits but dispersed costs. Government intervention in the sugar market provides a classic example of the principle. The federal government restricts importation of sugar and guarantees a minimum price to domestic sugar producers. Sugar producers employ only about 60,000 people in the entire country. The majority of the money from government payments for sugar goes to a small number of very large producers. In the mid 1990s, two Florida sugar producers were each receiving payments of over $50 million per year. The U.S. General Accounting Office estimated that sugar policy cost consumers a total of $1.9 billion in 1999, not including the money the government spent trying to clean up pollution in the Everglades caused by sugar farming. Unlike the benefits of the sugar policy, though, the costs are spread out over the entire U.S. population, so each person pays only about $20 per year and most people do not even know that they are paying it.

The case of sugar policy, and other policies like it, does not mean that the government never passes legislation that is in the public interest. These cases do, however, suggest that politicians sometimes pass laws that benefit special interest groups at the expense of most of the public. Such laws are particularly harmful to economic growth because they result in an inefficient use of resources. The laws create an incentive for businesses to use resources to lobby for special laws rather than to produce goods and services. Economists call such activities rent-seeking.

EVOLUTION OF STATE AND FEDERAL REGULATION

The roles of local, state, and federal government in the United States evolved over time as the economy changed. Overall, there has been a shift of responsibilities from state and local governments to the federal government.

During most of the nineteenth century, state and local governments bore most of the responsibility for economic regulation and for promotion of economic growth. State and local governments took an early and active role in promoting commerce. They provided support for roads, canals, and later railroads. The federal government played a smaller role in transport projects until the 1860s, when it began to provide large land grants to support the creation of an intercontinental railroad. States also played the leading role in promoting American financial development by chartering banks.

In the late nineteenth century, regulation of the economy began to shift toward the federal government. The Interstate Commerce Act of 1887 created the Interstate Commerce Commission, to regulate railroad rates. In 1890, the Sherman Antitrust Act was enacted to regulate monopolies. In 1904 the Pure Food and Drug Act established the Food and Drug Administration. In 1914 the Clayton Act was passed, the Fair Trade Commission was established, and the Sixteenth Amendment was enacted, making it possible for Congress to enact a federal income tax. In 1914 the federal government took a huge step in the direction of regulating finance in the national economy by creating the Federal Reserve as the nation's central bank.

During the Great Depression, direct federal government involvement in the economy increased markedly. Acts of Congress established the Securities and Exchange Commission, the Federal Deposit Insurance Corporation, the Federal Communication Commission, the Civil Aeronautics Board, and the National Labor Relations Board. The federal government took on the role of insuring people against poverty, particularly in old age. The Social Security Act made the federal government the insurer of last resort.

The Supreme Court facilitated the expansion of federal regulation by expanding the interpretation of the commerce clause. The "commerce clause" (Article 1, Section 8 of the Constitution) grants Congress the authority to regulate commerce "among the several states." In 1894 the Supreme Court ruled that the Sherman Antitrust Act could not be used against a sugar manufacturer because the manufacturer was involved only in production and not in commerce. But by the middle of the twentieth century, the Supreme Court concluded in *American Power and Lighting Company v. SEC* that the commerce clause gave Congress powers as "broad as the economic needs of the nation." The Supreme Court adopted the principle that the federal government could regulate anything that in any way affected interstate commerce, even if the activity appeared to take place within one state.

The broad interpretation of the commerce clause was prerequisite for the expansion of federal economic regulation that took place in the 1960s and 1970s. During these decades Congress created regulatory bodies that had discretion over broad socioeconomic issues: the Environmental Protection Agency to regulate pollution, the Consumer Product Safety Commission to regulate product safety, the Equal Employment Opportunity Commission to regulate discrimination.

The 1980s and 1990s saw some reversal of the trend toward increased federal regulation of the economy. Economists found that many types of industry regulation restricted new entry and competition and raised prices. The regulation served the firms in the regulated industry rather than consumers. Industry deregulation commenced under the Carter administration, but was taken further by the Reagan administration. From 1978 through 1999, federal legislation was passed to deregulate natural gas, trucking, telecommunications, savings and loans, banking, and airlines.

Ironically, although the Reagan administration sought to reduce the role of the federal government, the number of people employed by the federal

TABLE 7.2
Government Employment, 1980–2000 (in thousands)

Year	Fed	State	Local	Total	% Federal
1980	2,898	3,753	9,562	16,213	18
1990	3,105	3,105	10,760	16,970	18
2000	2,899	4,818	12,689	20,406	14

Source: U.S. Census Bureau, *Statistical Abstract of the United States, 2004–2005*; Table No. 453, Government Employment and Payrolls, 1980–2002.

government grew through the 1980s. Table 7.2 shows the number of people employed by the different levels of government in 1980, 1990, and 2000. Note that since 1990 the number of people employed by the federal government has fallen. On the other hand, the number of people employed by state and local governments has grown so rapidly that the total number of people employed by government has actually increased. These changes may mark a move back to a larger role for state and local governments.

Eight

The International Sector
and the National Economy

In February 2004, N. Gregory Mankiw was arguably the most influential economist in the United States. He was a professor at Harvard, author of the leading college economics textbook, and chief economist at the White House. Then he announced that moving service jobs overseas, called "outsourcing," is probably good for the economy in the long run because it results in cheaper goods and services for consumers. He said, "Outsourcing is just a new way of doing international trade."

Not surprisingly, Democrats who opposed President Bush's economic policies attacked the statement. But within the week even the Republican leader of the House of Representatives, Dennis Hastert, declared that Mankiw's "theory fails a basic test of real economics." President Bush distanced himself from Mankiw's statement.

There exists no bigger gap between the thoughts of economists and noneconomists than on international trade. Nearly all economists, like Mankiw, support free trade in outputs and in resources. Many Americans, and the politicians who represent them, are skeptical of the benefits of free trade and think that protecting jobs should be the first priority of trade policy. Americans are not alone. People in other countries also tend to be skeptical of the benefits of trade.

Concern with international trade grows as the importance of international trade to the American economy grows. Trade (imports plus exports) increased from 9 percent of U.S. GDP in 1959 to 25 percent of GDP in 2004. In 2004 the trade deficit (exports minus imports) was 5 percent of GDP.

The importance of trade to the rest of the world economy is even greater. From 1960 to 2001, trade as a percentage of total world GDP increased from 16 percent to 40 percent. The increasing relative importance of the international sector in the world economy is called "globalization." Opponents of globalization have a number of criticisms of free trade.

BARRIERS TO TRADE

Free trade is the absence of barriers to international trade. The most common barrier to trade is tariffs. Tariffs are taxes on imports or exports. Tariffs placed on imports make them more expensive relative to domestically produced goods. A second barrier to trade is quotas. Quotas are restrictions on the number of units of a good that can be imported. A third way to create a barrier to trade is through regulations, for example, requiring inspection of imported goods, which raise the costs of imports relative to domestic products.

The policy of erecting barriers to trade is called protectionism. The goal of protectionism is to insulate domestic producers from international market forces. Protectionism reduces the overall supply of the protected good, increasing the price that consumers pay. Protectionism also increases the share of total supply that is provided by domestic producers, increasing domestic production and employment.

Opponents of globalization and free trade offer several justifications for protectionism. The justification that is widely heard in the United States today is that protectionism saves jobs. A second justification is that protectionism really protects the U.S. from so-called "unfair" competition. Recently, opponents of globalization have expanded the "unfair" competition justification to argue that free trade exploits workers in less developed countries. A third justification is that free trade leads to large trade deficits and that large trade deficits are bad for the economy.

Economists argue that the benefits of free trade—which include lower prices, higher productivity, and higher real incomes—are large and widespread. In contrast, the benefits of protection are concentrated on specific groups at the expense of the general public. Because protectionism imposes costs on consumers and confers benefits on producers, it belongs to the class of redistributive economic policies discussed in chapter 7. Most economists believe that the costs of protectionism outweigh the benefits. In the view of most economists, protectionism is often good politics but bad economics.

THE BENEFITS OF TRADE

Even the most vigorous opponents of free trade accept that America should import some goods. For instance, it is acceptable to import agricultural products that are grown in the tropical regions of the world, such as bananas, cocoa, and coffee. Of course, most tropical produce can be grown in some parts of the United States, but it is very costly. Labor and other resources have to be diverted from more productive areas.

The argument that allows for importing tropical produce is precisely the argument for free trade generally. We should buy from other countries the goods that they can produce more cheaply than we can. With trade, we get the imported goods more cheaply than if they are produced domestically. Moreover, we are more productive when we do not have to devote our resources to producing things that we are not good at.

Ever since the English economist David Ricardo published *Principles of Political Economy and Taxation* in 1814, economists have used simple examples with two countries and two goods to illustrate the benefits of free trade. The hypothetical story is a long way from reality, but it makes it easier to see the benefits of trade than trying to consider all countries and all goods at the same time.

Imagine that the United States and Canada each have 100 million workers, and that each country produces only two goods: wheat and cars. If an American works in manufacturing, he can produce three cars per year. If he is in agriculture, he can produce five tons of wheat. If a Canadian works in manufacturing, she can produce one car per year. If she is in agriculture, she can produce five tons of wheat.

The countries can allocate workers however they want. They can decide to employ a few in agriculture and many in manufacturing or the other way around. In the absence of trade, each country has to employ some of its workers in manufacturing and some of its workers in agriculture in order to have both cars and wheat. Let us say that, in the absence of trade, each country allocates half of its workers to manufacturing and half to agriculture.

The result of dividing workers equally between the activities is shown in the first row of Table 8.1. Each country produces 250 million tons of grain. The United States produces 150 million cars, and Canada produces 50 million cars.

When a worker in the United States produces his five tons of grain, we give up production of the three cars he could have produced. When Canada uses a worker to produce five tons of grain, it gives up just one car. Even though Americans and Canadians are equally productive in agriculture, wheat is more costly to produce in the United States because we sacrifice more car production. In other words, the opportunity cost of producing wheat in the United States is higher than the opportunity cost of producing wheat in Canada. This implies that the United States is relatively better at producing cars.

TABLE 8.1
The Benefits of Trade

	Wheat for United States	Wheat for Canada	Cars for United States	Cars for Canada
No Trade–No Specialization	250 million	250 million	150 million	50 million
Specialization–No Trade	0	500 million	300 million	0
Specialization and Trade	250 million	250 million	175 million	125 million

Suppose the United States specializes in the production of cars, and Canada specializes in the production of wheat. The results of specialization are shown in the second horizontal row of Table 8.1. It is important to note that total production increases with specialization. The sum of wheat produced by the United States and Canada together remains at 500 million tons but the total number of cars produced by Canada and the United States together has increased from 200 million (150 by the United States and 50 million by Canada) to 300 million (all produced in the United States).

Because of the increase in total production, it is possible for Canada and the United States to trade so that each country has at least as much of each good as it did before it specialized and more of one of the goods. The third row of Table 8.1 shows one possible trade: The United States trades 125 million cars for 250 million tons of grain. Both Canada and the United States end up with more cars and as much wheat as they had before. Each country is better off with trade than without trade. Each country is able to benefit from trade because each is able to increase the total amount of goods produced by using resources more efficiently.

This is really just another version of the story about the benefits of trade presented in chapter 1. We are all better off from trading with each other than from trying to be self-sufficient. We can specialize in doing what we are good at and then trade with others. We do not have to waste our time trying to do things that we are not good at.

The same logic applies to trade between countries. It is possible to grow coffee in the United States, but our resources are much better suited to growing other crops. If we try to grow a little coffee, we have to give up a lot of the crop that the land and labor could have produced. Specialization and free trade enable us all to use our resources where they are most productive, and to enjoy the fruits of productive efforts elsewhere in the world.

Coffee is one of many commodities produced in the developing world and exported globally.

THE COST OF PROTECTION TO CONSUMERS

If we tried to grow coffee in the United States, we would end up paying more for a pound of coffee, and more for the crops given up to produce it. We all pay for protectionism by paying higher prices for goods and services. The average American household pays an additional $21 a year for sugar and products containing sugar because of restrictions on sugar imports. Similarly, the average household pays higher prices to protect the steel, and clothing, and lumber, and tuna industries. The list of protected items goes on and on. The Institute for International Economics estimated the cost of protectionism at $6,000 per household in the late 1990s. For comparison, in 2005, a single person with an income of $29,000 paid about $4,000 in income taxes.

JOB LOSS FROM PROTECTION

Few are aware of how much they pay for protectionism, and even fewer are aware of the jobs that are *lost* because of protectionism. Protectionism raises the prices of goods that are used as inputs by American firms to produce their own products. For these firms, protection raises the cost of production. A higher cost of production reduces supply and employment by the firms. For example, about 200,000 jobs were lost in steel-using industries due to protection of steel in 2002. Fewer than 200,000 people are employed in steel production in the United States. The higher cost of production, of course, also raises the price of the product. In some cases, firms that use protected products as inputs find their own exports reduced because of protectionism.

TRADE AND JOB LOSS

No one who supports free trade should make the mistake of suggesting that it makes everyone better off right away. Preventing imports through tariffs and quotas and other barriers is not called "protectionism" for nothing. It protects certain people, and when the protection is removed, those people are hurt.

It is true that removing protection causes some people to lose their jobs. Consider the simple example above, in which Canada and the United States produce wheat and cars. In the example, we assumed it was easy to switch people from wheat production to car production. In real life it is difficult. Farmers live in rural areas, not in cities where the cars are made. It may be difficult for them to leave their old lives behind and move to a new place. They may experience a long period of unemployment as they move from one job to another. They do not have any experience in automobile manufacturing, so although they may have a lot of work experience on the farm, they may have to start in an entry-level position at the factory.

Table 8.2 shows how many jobs are saved by protectionism in a few industries. The table also shows the cost of saving a job in each industry. Recall that the average American household pays $21 to protect sugar producers. Protection saves 2,261 jobs in the sugar industry at a cost of

TABLE 8.2
Cost of Saving Jobs

Industry	Jobs Saved	Total Cost (millions $s)	Cost per Job
Benzenoid chemicals	216	$297	$1,376,435
Luggage	226	290	1,285,078
Softwood lumber	605	632	1,044,271
Sugar	2,261	1,868	826,104
Polyethylene resins	298	242	812,928
Dairy products	2,378	1,630	685,323
Apparel and textiles	168,786	33,629	199,241

Source: G. C. Hufbauer and K. A. Elliott, *Measuring the Costs of Protection in the United States* (Washington, D.C.: Institute for International Economics, 1994), pp. 11–13.

$826,104 per job. If that seems like a lot to pay each year to save a job, then consider the benzenoid chemicals, luggage, and softwood lumber industries. Protection saves a little over 1,000 jobs in these industries at a cost of over a $1 million per job per year. Saving jobs through protection does not come cheap.

While the jobs saved by protectionism are significant to the individual workers who do not have to look for new jobs, protectionism has no noticeable impact on overall employment. Despite the fact that the share of trade in the American economy has increased by 16 percentage points since 1960, the unemployment rate in the early 2000s is practically the same as it was in the early 1960s. Job loss due to foreign trade does not affect overall unemployment because it is a very small part of overall job loss. In the early 2000s, around 15 million jobs were lost in each year. About 2 percent were lost due to foreign trade.

At the same time, about 15 million new jobs were created each year. The turnover of jobs, as some are created and some are destroyed, is called churn. The term churn is also used to describe the turnover of businesses as some fail and others are created. Churn, of course, means to stir things up. It is an essential part of economic growth. As new products and new processes are introduced into the economy, resources must be moved from one place to another to take advantage of the innovations.

Every year far more people lose jobs because of technological change than because of changes in trade flows. More often than not, lost jobs are not lost to outsourcing overseas, they are eliminated by innovations that increase productivity. From 1995 to 2002, the U.S. textile industry lost 202,000 jobs. If these jobs were outsourced to take advantage of cheap labor in China, it does not show up in Chinese employment figures. The Chinese textile industry lost 1.8 million jobs during the same period.

Manufacturing employment in the United States began declining in the late 1970s. The decline in manufacturing employment is sometimes used to imply that manufacturing has become less important in the American economy. Nothing could be further from the truth. The Federal Reserve's index of manufacturing production increased from 57 in 1980 to 112 in 2003. That is, the production of manufactured goods almost doubled while the number of people employed in manufacturing declined. American manufacturing has not moved overseas. It has gotten more productive. We no longer need so many people to produce our manufactured goods; their labor has been freed up to do other things.

In the past, people opposed technological change because it cost people their jobs. During the Industrial Revolution, Luddites (followers of the fictional Ned Ludd) smashed textile machines. Such opposition to technology is not widely accepted today because people see the obvious benefits of technological improvement. People accept that some workers are displaced as a result of technological progress.

In the end, technological change and foreign trade have the same threefold impact. They allow us to use our resources more productively; they lower the cost of goods; they cause people to have to switch jobs.

EXPLOITING THE POOR

People sometimes support protection but say they are for "fair trade" or a "level playing field." They argue that free trade is not fair because other countries have lower costs of labor or less regulation than in the United States. They claim that globalization exploits the poor. Some go so far as to argue that free trade makes poor countries poorer, and that multinational corporations that use labor in developing countries should be boycotted. The argument that free trade exploits the poor suffers from several flaws.

The fundamental flaw with the argument that free trade is being used to exploit workers in less developed countries is that it fails to explain why people voluntarily take low-paying jobs in factories. People choose the factory jobs because they are better than the alternatives. For many factory workers in less developed countries, the only alternative is an even lower paying job and harder work in agriculture.

Close examination of the international sector reveals other flaws. If businesses care mainly about the availability of cheap labor when they decide where to build factories, then investment into the poorest of the poor countries would be large, and exports from the poorest of the poor countries would be large as well. The poorest countries and the lowest wages in the world are in Africa. Few businesses move into Africa to take advantage of the low wages there. Table 8.3 shows flows of foreign direct investment from the United States into other countries. Businesses headquartered in the United States sent more investment dollars to the country of Denmark in 2003 than they did to the entire continent of Africa.

In fact, most international investment flows back and forth between the most developed countries in the world. Of the $1,167,337 million in foreign direct investment in the world in 2001, more than 86 percent went to high-income countries, countries that account for less than one-sixth of world population but produce five-sixths of world income. A little more than one-half of 1 percent of foreign direct investment went to the low-income countries, countries that account for one-third of world population and had an average per capita GDP of $430 that year. The low-income countries accounted for

TABLE 8.3
Foreign Direct Investment Position, 2003

Country	U.S. Investment in (millions $s)	Country	Investment in United States (millions $s)
United Kingdom	272,140	United Kingdom	218,175
Canada	192,409	Japan	159,160
Netherlands	178,933	Netherlands	153,679
Switzerland	86,435	France	141,400
Africa	18,960	Africa	2,298

Source: U.S. Census Bureau, *Statistical Abstract of the United States, 2004–2005;* Table No. 1283, Foreign Direct Investment Position in the United States on a Historical-Cost Basis by Industry and Selected Country: 1990 to 2003; and Table No. 1288, U.S. Direct Investment Position Abroad on a Historical-Cost Basis by Selected Country: 1990 to 2003.

only 3.5 percent of world exports. The "globalized" world is the world of the high-income countries, not the world of the low-income countries.

If low wages and desire to avoid regulation are the driving forces in the international sector, then Madagascar and Zimbabwe should be among leading exporters to the United States. They are not. Table 8.4 shows the major trading partners of the United States. The most obvious fact about international trade, in fact, is that most trade occurs between the same few rich countries. The only difference between the top ten countries we export to and the top ten countries we import from is that Ireland is on the import list but not the export list, and Netherlands is on the export list but not the import list.

TABLE 8.4
America's Top Trading Partners

Export Purchasers	Import Suppliers
Canada	Canada
Mexico	China
Japan	Mexico
United Kingdom	Japan
Germany	Germany
China	United Kingdom
S. Korea	S. Korea
Netherlands	Taiwan
Taiwan	France
France	Ireland

Source: U.S. Census Bureau, *Statistical Abstract of the United States, 2004–2005;* Figure 28.2, Top Purchasers of U.S. Exports and Suppliers of U.S. General Imports: 2003.

Protecting Infant Industry

An argument called the "infant industry" argument was used in the nine-teenth century to support protectionist tariffs and is still sometimes used today. The argument asserts that a firm, like an infant, needs protection when it is young. As the firm produces more of its product, it learns better ways to produce and costs fall. Eventually the new firm can compete with older, more established firms and protection can be removed. The applica-tion of the infant industry argument poses difficulties. First, the government must decide which infants need protection. Second, the government must decide when an industry has grown up enough so that protection can safely be removed. Finally, the government must develop a way to encourage an infant industry to increase productivity and lower its costs in the absence of the threat of competition.

If American firms were unable to compete internationally, then the trade deficit would be the result of a lack of demand for U.S. products, implying a decline in U.S. exports, but exports have risen to record levels in the past decades. American firms compete especially well in the services sector, where we consistently run trade surpluses.

THE BALANCE OF PAYMENTS

The large trade deficits of the United States are sometimes blamed on free trade. To see whether free trade causes deficits, we must first look carefully at what the trade deficit is.

Just as the federal government tries to estimate the size of the U.S. economy using its national income accounts, it tries to measure our economic relations with the rest of the world in the balance of payments. The balance of pay-ments tracks everything that results in a demand for U.S. dollars or a supply of U.S. dollars. Each transaction between a party in the United States and a party abroad creates a demand for, or a supply of, U.S. dollars. If a car dealer in Germany wants to import cars made in America, he has to buy U.S. dollars in order to purchase them. If an American wants to buy a car made in Germany, she needs to sell U.S. dollars to buy German marks.

Exchange Rates

Currencies are bought and sold on the foreign exchange market. In the absence of government interference, exchange rates are determined like any other market price: by supply and demand. The market for a currency is like the markets for resources (see chapter 6). Firms buy labor from households, not because labor is intrinsically valuable, but because firms need labor to produce output. Similarly, we do not demand foreign currency for its own sake. We demand foreign currency because we need it to buy things from other countries. The more a firm wants to produce, the more labor it demands. The more foreign things we want to buy, the more we demand the foreign currency.

When foreign exchange rates are determined by market prices, they are said to be "floating." "Fixed" exchange rates are determined by a country's government and do not change in response to changes in supply and demand. Some countries pursue a policy of a "managed float" with respect to exchange rates. A managed float exists when the value of the currency is generally determined by market forces, but the government sometimes intervenes when it thinks the exchange rate has gone too far in one direction or another. If market forces are driving up the price of the currency, the government increases supply of the currency to drive down the price. If market forces are driving down the price, the government increases demand to drive up the price.

Whenever we state a foreign exchange rate, we are actually stating two prices. For example, the exchange rate between the British pound and the U.S. dollar states the price of the pound in terms of dollars, and it also states the price of the dollars in terms of pounds.

Sometimes people talk about having a "strong" dollar. There is, however, no absolute standard by which to evaluate foreign exchange rates. We can only compare exchange rates today to what they were in the past. If the dollar buys more euros than it did last month, then the dollar is stronger relative to the euro. Another way of saying this is that the dollar appreciated against the euro. If the dollar buys fewer euros, then we say that the dollar has depreciated.

Appreciation of the dollar is good news for people going abroad. Again, buying things in foreign countries is a two-step process. First we buy the currency of the country, then we buy the things we want. If we travel to England, we need to buy pounds to buy our fish and chips. The more expensive pounds are, the more the good costs in dollars. If lunch costs £5 and each pound costs $2, then lunch costs $10. But if each pound costs only $1, then lunch only costs $5. By the same logic, a stronger dollar is good for people in the United States who want to import goods.

Appreciation of the dollar against the pound is bad news for the British traveler and the American tourist industry. With the weaker dollar, each pound buys $2, and a $10 lunch in the United States only costs £5. When the dollar is stronger, each pound buys only $1, and a $10 lunch costs

£10. Appreciation is bad for British who wish to import from the United States.

In addition to imports of goods and services, people buy assets from people in other countries. Buying stocks or bonds in another country, or buying actual physical assets like a farm or a factory, also requires that we have the currency of that country first.

Recognizing that there are two demands for foreign currency, one to buy goods and services and the other to buy assets, helps us understand how the balance of payments works.

THE CURRENT AND CAPITAL ACCOUNTS

The balance of payments has two sides. The first side measures the flow of goods and services. This side is called the current account. The current account tracks imports, exports, income that is received from abroad, and income that is paid out to people in other countries. The oft-referred-to trade deficit is a current account deficit. When a country buys more goods from the rest of the world than it sells to the rest of the world, it runs a current account deficit. When it sells more goods to the rest of the world than it buys from the rest of the world, it runs a current account surplus.

The second side measures the flow of financial resources. This side is called the capital account. The capital account tracks flows of financial assets, such as purchases of stocks and bonds. When a country sells more assets to the rest of the world than it buys from the rest of the world, it runs a current account deficit. A current account surplus is a net inflow of financial resources. A current account deficit is a net outflow of financial resources. The media tends to pay much less attention to the capital account, and people are consequently less familiar with it, but the capital account and the current account are inseparable.

When there is a deficit on the current account, there must be a surplus on the capital account. If businesses in the United States sell more goods to the rest of the world than foreign businesses sell to firms in the United States, people in the United States must lend the rest of the world an amount equal to the difference so they have enough dollars to pay for the goods they want.

When there is a surplus on the current account, there must be a deficit on the capital account. If businesses in the United States buy more from businesses in the rest of the world than foreign businesses buy from the United States, Americans must borrow the difference from the rest of the world so we have enough of other currencies to pay for the goods we want.

If consumption, government spending, or investment in the United States goes up, interest rates go up in the United States. Purchasing a U.S.

Currency Crises

Political unrest or reports of corruption cause a loss of confidence on the part of foreign investors. If foreign investors lose confidence, they sell off the assets they hold and take their money out of a country. For example, if investors lose confidence in their Mexican investments because of reports of bribes, they sell the stocks they own in Mexican businesses and convert the pesos into dollars. Selling pesos drives down the value of the peso, which makes it even less attractive to keep money in Mexico. More people sell their Mexican assets. People rush to get rid of pesos before their value falls even more. The result is a currency crisis. While depreciation does make exports more attractive, rapid depreciation makes foreigners unwilling to invest in businesses in a country. Lower investment is bad for long-term growth.

---

asset like a bond becomes more attractive to foreign investors. To purchase a bond, a foreign investor first has to purchase dollars. The increase in demand for dollars causes the dollar to appreciate. The appreciation of the dollar causes U.S. goods and services to become less affordable to foreign buyers, and U.S. exports decline. Thus we have foreigners lending us more, but buying fewer of our products.

The same story can be initiated by forces from abroad. If the United States becomes a more attractive place to invest relative to other countries because of political and economic stability, then foreigners invest more in the United States. The strong demand for U.S. assets keeps U.S. interest rates down, but the strong demand for U.S. currency keeps its price up, making U.S. exports less attractive.

THE CAUSES OF TRADE DEFICITS

Trade deficits are not determined by other countries' tariffs or quotas, or other countries' low wages, or other governments' regulations. What determines whether we run a trade deficit or a trade surplus is the relationship between the amount of goods and services we produce in a year and the amount of goods and services that we choose to consume. If U.S. households, U.S. businesses, and the U.S. government together choose to consume less than we produce, we run a trade surplus. If we choose to consume more than we produce, we run a trade deficit. I repeat for emphasis: The trade balance is the result of the choices made by people within a country, not by the choices of people outside the country.

Trade deficits cannot be eliminated by means of tariffs or quotas. Trade deficits can be eliminated only by choosing not to consume more than is produced. If the United States wants to eliminate its trade deficit, people in the United States must increase household savings or reduce the government budget deficit.

Are Trade Deficits Bad?

The United States has had a deficit in its current account for all but three years since 1977. The current period is not the only one of prolonged trade deficits. The United States also ran trade deficits in 25 out of 39 years from 1821 to 1860 and probably also in most of the years from 1789 to 1821. Both in the nineteenth century and now, the U.S. economy grew rapidly while running trade deficits.

The trade deficit, therefore, is not inherently a bad thing. If we run a trade deficit, it simply means that we are borrowing from abroad so that we can use more goods and services than we produce. Whether or not an excess of consumption over production is a good thing depends on what we consume. If we borrow from abroad to finance investments that make us more productive in the future, trade deficits are good for long-run growth. On the other hand, if borrowing from abroad is not profitably invested, then it is hard to argue that the borrowing is a good idea.

Consider the case of Congo (formerly Zaire). The dictator Mobuto Sese Seko borrowed money from abroad to finance his own personal consumption. Since the trade deficit did not enhance the ability of Congo to produce goods and services, it was probably not a good policy.

Trade deficits for a country are not much different than the life cycle of borrowing and savings for an individual (see chapter 6). Most of us go through a long period in our youth during which we behave like a country running a trade deficit. From the time we are born until the time we leave school and get a full-time job, we consume more each year than we produce. We are able to do this because we receive aid from our parents, grandparents, or someone else (such as the bank that makes our student loans). Our parents and grandparents are like countries with trade surpluses. They produce more than they use during a year and choose to invest their surpluses in us.

IMMIGRATION

We have looked at international flows of goods and services and flows of financial resources. People also flow across international borders. Figure 8.1 shows immigration to the United States since 1820.

The United States is a nation of immigrants. In the eighteenth and nineteenth centuries, the flow of immigrants was relatively free of barriers.

FIGURE 8.1
Immigration, 1820–2000

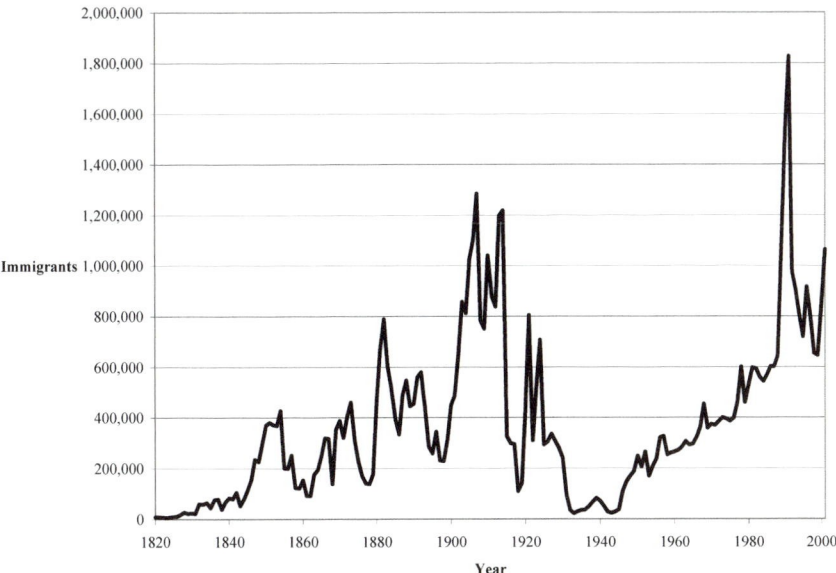

Source: http://uscis.gov/graphics/shared/aboutus/statistics/index.htm; and U.S. Census Bureau, *Historical Statistics of the United States, Colonial Period To 1970;* Series C 89–119, Immigrants by Country: 1820 to 1970.

Early in American history, the cost of travel was the most significant impediment to immigration. Large numbers of people emigrated to the United States—they first came from Great Britain, then, especially after the 1840s, they came from Ireland, Germany, and other parts of Northern Europe.

The Chinese Exclusion Act of 1882 was the first legal barrier to the flow of immigration to the United States. Public response to a new wave of immigration from Southern and Eastern Europe in the early twentieth century led Congress to pass additional restrictions on immigration in the 1920s. Not until the 1980s did the numbers of immigrants to the United States reach the levels that it had in the early twentieth century.

Immigrants contribute to U.S. output by bringing their labor to the United States. In addition, immigrants bring useful knowledge and entrepreneurial talent. Samuel Slater brought knowledge about cotton-spinning machinery. Andrew Carnegie emigrated from Scotland and built Carnegie Steel into what would become the first billion-dollar corporation. Albert Einstein, Enrico Fermi, and John von Neumann enriched the American scientific community.

Opposition to immigration, like opposition to trade, usually focuses on a presumed loss of jobs. However, immigration has little impact on labor markets. Refer again to Figure 8.1. Immigration rose sharply in the 1990s, reaching its highest levels ever, yet unemployment fell in the 1990s to its lowest levels in over thirty years. The evidence indicates that demand for labor in our growing economy increases faster than supply, even with immigration.

The international sector is often cast in the role of the villain. But trade and immigration are not threats to the American economy. The international sector provides the United States with labor, knowledge, and financial resources to increase our capital stock and enhance our long-run economic growth.

Sources of Current Economic Information

There are a number of useful resources for staying informed about the economy. The business section of most newspapers generally reports the latest data on unemployment, inflation and production, as well as reporting daily on stock markets and important economic events. In addition, a number of sources are available for people who wish to study economic issues in more detail.

FEDERAL GOVERNMENT SOURCES

One of the most useful sources of information on the economy is the *Statistical Abstract of the United States* published every year by the Census Bureau and available online at the Census Bureau's website at http://www.census.gov/. The *Statistical Abstract* covers production, income, education, population, telecommunications, vital statistics, manufacturing, foreign trade, and numerous other topics. Recent editions contain over a thousand tables. Because it is a compilation, the *Statistical Abstract* does not usually contain the most up-to-date information, however, each chapter begins with a clear description of the sources of the data, what they mean, how they are collected, and where they can be obtained. One can find the most up-to-date statistics by following these leads.

Longtime series of many economic variables can be found in United States, Census Bureau, *Historical Statistics of the United States from the Colonial Period To 1970*. A new edition of *Historical Statistics of the United States* was published by Cambridge University Press in 2005.

A very convenient source of current information on the economy is the White House's Economic Statistics Briefing Room available online at http://www.whitehouse.gov/fsbr/esbr.html.

The White House also publishes *The Economic Report of the President* every year. In addition to containing analysis of the current state of the economy, *The Economic Report of the President* contains numerous tables on macroeconomic variables. Most of these tables are time series dating back to 1959. *The Economic Report of the President* is available in print form and online through the Government Printing Office website at http://a257.g.akamai tech.net/7/257/2422/17feb20051700/www.gpoaccess.gov/eop/index.html. The online tables can be downloaded in Excel format and are thus particularly useful for people who wish to do their own analysis or develop their own charts and tables.

The Department of Labor's Bureau of Labor Statistics provides the most current information on employment, productivity, prices, and labor costs. Their website is located at www.bls.gov.

The primary source of information on GDP and national income as well as all of their components is the Department of Commerce, Bureau of Economic Analysis. Estimates of GDP and national income are published in *Survey of Current Business*, which is available in a printed format at many libraries as well as online at http://www.bea.doc.gov/bea/glance.htm.

THE FEDERAL RESERVE SYSTEM

The Federal Reserve is the primary source of information about money, credit, and interest rates. In addition, the Fed reports on many other economic variables such as industrial production. The principal publication is the *Federal Reserve Bulletin*, available in print and online at www.federalreserve.gov. Numerous statistics are available through the Fed on its Statistics: Releases and Historical Data web page located at http://www.federalreserve.gov/releases/.

In addition, each of the Federal Reserve banks has its own website. These websites are highly useful for people who want to understand the economy. The Reserve banks are strong proponents of economic education, and their websites usually contain a great deal of information presented in a non-technical fashion.

The easiest way to find the website of the Fed nearest you is to use an Internet search engine. Typically, they have obvious addresses such as:
the Federal Reserve Bank of St. Louis (http://www.stlouisfed.org/);
the Federal Reserve Bank of Dallas (http://www.dallasfed.org/);
and the Federal Reserve Bank of San Francisco (http://www.frbsf.org/).

INTERNATIONAL STATISTICS

Two annual publications present economic statistics for most countries in the world. The World Bank publishes *World Development Report*, and the United Nations publishes *Human Development Report*.

PRIVATE ORGANIZATIONS

A number of think tanks publish analyses of current economic events in a manner that is accessible to noneconomists. Much of their research is available free of charge and online.

The Cato Institute, www.cato.org.

The Brookings Foundation, www.brook.edu.

The Independent Institute, www.independent.org.

Institute for International Economics, www.iie.org.

The American Enterprise Institute, www.aei.org.

Economic Policy Institute, epinet.org.

Urban Institute, www.urban.org.

Finally, the American Economic Association has web page of Resources for Economists developed by Bill Goffe. Resources for Economists provides direction to a wide range of Internet sites of use to anyone interested in economic issues, at http://www.aeaweb.org/RFE/.

Glossary

Aggregate demand. The total planned spending on newly produced goods and services throughout the economy.

Antitrust policy. Policies to prevent monopoly and unfair trade practices, and promote competition.

Automatic stabilizers. Changes in government expenditures and taxes that take place automatically as the economy expands or contracts.

Balance of payments. A summary of transactions with the rest of the world during a given period of time.

Balanced budget. A situation in which outlays exactly equal revenue. Sometimes used to refer to a situation in which outlays do not exceed revenues.

Barriers to entry. Factors that make it very difficult for new firms to enter a market.

Barter. Trading things without the use of money.

Basis point. One one-hundredth of a percentage point.

Board of governors, of the Federal Reserve. Seven people appointed by the president to lead the Fed. Appointments are for fourteen years. All governors serve on the FOMC.

Bond. A promise to repay a debt, in specific amounts at specific dates.

Budget. A plan stating expected revenues and outlays during a specific period of time.

Budget deficit. The difference between revenue and outlays when spending exceeds revenue.

Bureau of Economic Analysis. The division of the Department of Commerce responsible for national income and product accounting.

CAFTA. Central American Free Trade Agreement. Agreement to lower trade barriers among the United States and Central American countries.

Capital. (1) Things that are produced to be used as inputs in the production of more things in the future. Human capital is embodied in people. Physical capital is embodied in things. (2) Sometimes also used to refer to financial resources.

Capital account. The part of the balance of payments that tracks flows of assets with the rest of the world.

Capital gain. The increase in the price of an asset.

Capitalism. An economic system in which people own most of society's resources and voluntarily trade goods and services with each other in markets.

Chain weighting. Procedure used to adjust nominal values for changes in prices. The Bureau of Economic Analysis uses chain weighting to calculate real GDP.

Checkable deposits. Deposits that can be used as a medium of exchange by means of a check or debit card.

Classical economics. A view of the macroeconomy that emphasizes the stability of a market economy.

Clayton Act (1914). Antitrust legislation that forbids interlocking directorates and mergers that substantially reduce competition. Also provides for treble damages and states that labor is not subject to antitrust legislation.

Commerce clause. Article 1, Section 8 of the Constitution gives Congress the right to regulate commerce "among the several states." Also known as the interstate commerce clause. Provides the constitutional foundation for federal regulation of the economy.

Commercial bank. A bank that takes in deposits and makes loans.

Common stock. Stock with voting rights.

Comparative advantage. The activity that a person or nation can do at a lower opportunity cost than its trading partners.

Compensation. Wages plus non-wage benefits.

Consumer Price Index. A measure of the average level of prices for consumer goods. It is equal to 100 in the base year.

Core competency. The thing that a business does best.

Core inflation. The rate of inflation excluding food and energy prices.

Corporation. A form of business organization in which stockholders with limited liability are the owners.

Creative destruction. The process by which innovation increases productivity but makes old capital and technology obsolete.

Crowding out. The negative impact on investment that results when borrowing to finance increased government spending causes interest rates to rise.

Current account. The part of the balance of payments that tracks flows of goods and services with the rest of the world.

Cyclical unemployment. Unemployment caused by insufficient aggregate demand.

Deflation. A decrease in the general price level.

Demand. The quantity of a good or service that people in a market plan to purchase. Demand for a good or service depends on the price of the good or service, related prices, income, wealth, expectations, and the number of buyers. The total amount of demand in the economy is called the aggregate demand.

Depreciation. The reduction in the value of a piece of capital over time as it wears out.

Depression. Unusually severe recession. Usually reserved for the Great Depression (1930s) and the Depression of the 1890s.

Deregulation. Removal of regulatory rules for an industry.

Discount rate. (1) The interest rate that is used to convert future payments to a present value. (2) The rate of interest charged by the Federal Reserve for overnight loans.

Disposable income. Income minus tax payments.

Due process clause. Part of the Fifth and Fourteenth Amendments that declares that life, liberty, and property cannot be taken without due process of law.

Earnings. (1) Profits of a corporation. (2) Wages.

Economics. The study of how people choose to allocate their scarce resources.

Economies of scale. Decreases in the average cost of production that result from increasing the size of the production facility.

Employment Act of 1946. Requires the federal government to try to maintain maximum employment, sustained growth, and stable prices. Also established the Council of Economic Advisers for the president and the Joint Economic Committee of the Congress, and requires the president to prepare an *Economic Report of the President*.

Entrepreneur. A person who introduces an innovation: a new resource, a new market, a new product, or a new method of production.

Equilibrium. A situation in which there is no tendency for change to occur. In economics, equilibrium occurs when people's plans all fit together.

Exchange rate. The price of one currency in terms of another.

Excise tax. Tax on a specific item.

Expectations. Beliefs about the future.

Expected inflation. The rate of inflation that people expect to exist in the future.

Expenditure multiplier. The process that causes a change in aggregate spending to become magnified because it induces further changes in consumption expenditures.

Externality. A type of market failure. A spillover of costs or benefits onto someone who was not involved in the choices that created the costs or benefits.

Federal Deposit Insurance Corporation. A corporation that insures deposits at commercial banks up to $100,000. The FDIC is intended to prevent bank runs by assuring people that they will not lose their deposits, even if the bank fails.

Federal funds rate. The rate of interest charged by banks to other banks for short-term loans.

Federal Trade Commission. Established in 1914 to regulate unfair competition and unfair and deceptive practices.

FICA. Federal Insurance Contribution Act. The name of the payroll tax for Social Security and Medicare.

Financial intermediary. Any firm that moves financial resources from suppliers to demanders.

Fiscal policy. The use of taxing and spending to try to influence the performance of the economy.

Fractional reserve banking. Banking system in which banks keep only a fraction of their deposits on reserve as cash in their vault or with another bank, and lend out the rest of the deposits at interest.

Free rider. A person who benefits from the goods or services purchased by someone else without paying for those benefits.

Frictional unemployment. Unemployment caused by people moving into the workforce or between jobs.

Friedman, Milton. (1912–) Nobel Prize–winning economist. Advocate of free markets and monetarism.

GDP deflator. Price index based on the entire GDP.

Gold standard. International monetary system in which countries stated a rate at which their currency exchanged for gold and required that all money be convertible to gold at that rate. The gold standard established fixed exchange rates, encouraging foreign trade and investment.

Government expenditures. Category of national income accounting. Purchases of newly produced goods and services by federal, state, and local governments. Not the same as outlays in government budgets. Government expenditure does not include transfer payments, which are included as part of outlays in the government budget.

Gross Domestic Product. The market value of final goods and services produced within a country during a given period of time, usually a year.

Human capital. Capital that is embodied in a human being. Learning that improves a person's productivity. Can come from formal education or experience.

Humphrey-Hawkins Act (1978). Set economic goals for the federal government including: maximum growth and employment, price stability, balanced budgets, and balanced trade.

Hyperinflation. Periods of very rapid inflation in which prices rise from thousands to trillions of times.

Incentives. The combination of benefits and costs associated with choices about the allocation of scarce resources.

Index number. A measuring device created by dividing the value of a basket of things by the value of that basket in a base period and then multiplying by 100. Used to measure changes in prices for the economy as a whole or in a stock market. Also used to measure changes in particular sectors of the economy, such as industrial production.

Index of Leading Economic Indicators. Compiled by the Conference Board based on changes in variables that tend to occur before changes in general economic activity.

Inflation. Percentage change in the overall price level during a period of time, often from one year to the next.

Initial public offering. The first offering of a corporation's stock to the general public.

Innovation. The introduction of a new good or service, new method of production, new resource, or new market.

Institutions. The rules of the game. Composed of formal rules, such as laws and regulations, and informal rules, such as social norms of behavior.

Interstate Commerce Act (1887). Established the Interstate Commerce Commission, the first federal regulatory agency, to regulate businesses engaged in transporting goods and people across state boundaries.

Investment. (1) A category of expenditure in the national income accounting framework that includes business purchases of newly produced capital, changes in business inventories, and residential construction. This is the meaning that is primarily used by economists. (2) The purchase of financial assets, such as stocks. This is the usage most common among noneconomists.

Keynes, John Maynard (1883–1946). English economist responsible for the development of the idea that recessions are caused by inadequate aggregate demand.

Keynesian economics. Approach to the macroeconomics that emphasizes aggregate demand, expectations, and inflexibility of wages and prices.

Labor force. The working-age population (16–65) that is either employed or unemployed.

Laissez-faire. Idea that government involvement in the economy should be minimal.

M1. Narrowest definition of the money supply. Includes currency, coins, travelers checks, and checkable deposits.

M2. Includes everything in M1 plus deposits that can easily be converted into M1, such as savings deposits and money market deposit accounts.

Macroeconomics. The branch of economics that studies the national economy as a whole.

Market. A place where buyers and sellers come together. Does not have to be an actual physical location.

Market economy. An economy in which most decisions about how to allocate goods and services are made by people interacting in markets.

Market failure. A situation in which markets may not work well because of externalities, public goods, or lack of competition.

Microeconomics. The branch of economics that studies individual firms and households and their interaction in markets.

Minimum wage. Lowest wage rate that an employer can legally pay.

Monetarism. An approach to macroeconomics that argues in support of increasing the money supply at a constant rate consistent with the long-run rate of growth of real output. Monetarists believe that attempts to actively manage the economy do more harm than good.

Monetary policy. The use of changes in the money supply to try to influence the performance of the economy.

Money. Anything that is generally accepted as a means of payment. Also known as a medium of exchange.

Money multiplier process. The process that causes initial changes in bank reserves to generate an increase in the money supply that is larger than the initial change in reserves.

Monopoly. The existence of a single firm in a market.

Monopoly power (market power). The ability of a firm to charge higher than competitive prices. Monopoly power is greater the less close substitutes there are for the firm's product.

NAFTA. North American Free Trade Agreement. Agreement to reduce trade barriers between Canada, the United States, and Mexico.

NAIRU. Non-Accelerating Inflation Rate of Unemployment. The lowest rate of unemployment that can be attained without inflation accelerating.

National Bureau of Economic Research. Private research organization founded in 1920.

National income. The market value of the income generated from production of final goods and services within a country during a given period of time.

National income and product account. The measurement of income and production at the national level. Contains estimates of GDP and its components and national income and its components.

Natural rate of output. Potential output. The output produced when unemployment is at the natural rate, or NAIRU.

Natural rate of unemployment. The rate of unemployment that exists when there is only frictional and structural unemployment.

Net exports. Exports minus imports.

Nominal. Economic variables measured in current prices.

North, Douglass C. (1921–). Nobel Prize–winning economist. Emphasized the role of institutions in shaping incentives and economic performance.

Open market operations. The buying and selling of government securities by the Federal Reserve to initiate changes in the money supply. Conducted by the Federal Reserve Bank of New York.

Opportunity cost. The value of the next best alternative that is given up when a choice is made.

Personal income. Income minus contributions for government social insurance programs.

Poverty rate. Percentage of households with income below the poverty line.

Present value. The discounted value of a future sum of money.

Productivity. (1) Output per unit of input. (2) Labor productivity. Output per unit of labor input. (3) Total factor productivity. Output per unit of all inputs (land, labor, and capital).

Profits. Revenue minus costs.

Progressive tax. A tax in which a person pays a higher percentage of income as their income rises.

Property rights. Legally enforceable rights to use, to alienate (sell, trade, or give away), and to receive income from property.

Protection (Protectionism). Tariffs, quotas, or other restraints on trade intended to raise the price of a good, protecting domestic producers and their employees from foreign competition.

Public goods. Goods that are nonrival and nonexcludable.

Purchasing power parity. The idea that a unit of currency should be able to buy the same amount of goods in each country.

Real GDP. GDP adjusted to eliminate the effect of increased prices.

Real interest rate. The nominal interest rate minus the rate of inflation.

Real wages. Nominal wages adjusted for changes in the price level.

Reserve requirement. The percentage of deposits that banks are required to keep in reserve as cash in their vault or as deposits with another bank.

Sarbanes-Oxley Act (2002). Legislation requiring improved reporting by corporations.

Savings. (1) The part of income that is not consumed. (2) In national income accounting, national savings is the sum of household savings, business savings, and government savings. (3) The increase in a household's wealth.

Securities and Exchange Commission. Agency established in 1934 to regulate the securities industry.

Sherman Act (1890). Foundation of American antitrust law. Forbids monopolies, attempts to monopolize, and contracts, combinations, and conspiracies in restraint of trade.

Smith, Adam (1723–90). Author of *Inquiry into the Nature and Causes of the Wealth of Nations* (1776). Regarded as the founder of modern economics.

Social Security. Name commonly used for Old Age, Survivors, Disability Insurance (OASDI).

Specialization and division of labor. The practice of having people specialize in particular tasks rather than having everyone trying to do everything. Adam Smith regarded it as the foundation for increasing production.

Stagflation. Period of both high unemployment and high inflation.

Stock. A share of ownership in a corporation.

Stock market. Market in which people buy and sell corporate stocks.

Structural unemployment. Unemployment that arises from structural changes in an economy, such as decline in demand for a product, technological change, or change in international trade.

Supply. The quantity of goods that sellers plan to sell. Supply depends on the price of the good, the price of inputs needed to produce the good, and the level of technology.

Takings clause. Clause of the Fifth Amendment that states that private property may not be taken for public use without just compensation. Applies not just to situations in which the property is physically taken, but also to situations in which government regulation takes away part of someone's property rights by drastically limiting what they can do with their property.

Tariffs. Taxes on imports or exports. In the United States, only tariffs on imports are allowed by the Constitution.

Taxes. Payments that people and corporations are required to make to the government, based on their income, wealth, or purchases.

Trade deficit. The current account deficit. The amount by which imports exceed exports.

Transaction costs. The cost of measuring, monitoring, and enforcing an exchange.

Transfer payments. Payments for which no good or service is received in exchange.

Unemployment rate. Percentage of the labor force that is unemployed.

Value-Added Tax (VAT). Tax on value added, widely used in Europe.

Velocity. The average number of times a dollar is used in a year. Equal to GDP divided by the money supply.

Wages. Payments for labor, generally on an hourly basis. In the past, wages were often expressed as daily rather than hourly.

WPI. Wholesale Price Index. Measure of the prices meant to represent what businesses typically purchase.

References

Atack, Jeremy, and Peter Passell. *A New Economic View of American History from Colonial Times to 1940*. 2d ed. New York: Norton, 1994.

Cox, W. Michael, and Richard Alm. *Myths of Rich and Poor: Why We're Better off Than We Think*. New York: Basic Books, 1999.

Easterlin, Richard. *Growth Triumphant: The Twenty-First Century in Historical Perspective*. Ann Arbor: University of Michigan Press, 1996.

Easterly, William. *The Elusive Quest for Growth: Economists' Adventures and Misadventures in the Tropics*. Cambridge: MIT Press, 2001.

Ferguson, Roger W., and William Wascher. "Distinguished Lecture on Economics in Government: Lessons from Past Productivity Booms." *Journal of Economic Perspectives* 18 (2004): 3–28.

Friedman, Milton, and Rose Friedman. *Free to Choose*. New York: Avon, 1979.

Helpman, Elhanan. *The Mystery of Economic Growth*. Cambridge: Belknap Press, 2004.

Koop, Todd A. *Recessions and Depressions: Understanding Business Cycles*. Westport, CT: Praeger, 2004.

Krugman, Paul. *The Age of Diminished Expectations*. 3d ed. Cambridge: MIT Press, 1997.

Layard, Richard. *Happiness: Lessons from a New Science*. New York: Penguin Press, 2005.

Maital, Shlomo. *Executive Economics: Ten Essential Tools for Managers*. New York: Free Press, 1994.

Mayer, Laurence. *A Term at the Fed: An Insider's View*. New York: HarperCollins, 2004.

McCloskey, Donald, ed. *Second Thoughts: Myths and Morals of U.S. Economic History*. New York: Oxford University Press, 1993.

McCraw, Thomas K. *American Business, 1920–2000: How It Worked*. Wheeling: Harlan Davidson, 2000.

McKenzie, Richard. *The Paradox of Progress: Can Americans Regain Their Confidence in a Prosperous Future?* New York: Oxford University Press, 1997.

Meulendyke, Ann-Marie. *U.S. Monetary Policy and Financial Markets.* New York: Federal Reserve Bank of New York, 1998.

Mokyr, Joel. *The Lever of Riches: Technological Creativity and Economic Progress.* New York: Oxford University Press, 1990.

———. "The Intellectual Origins of Modern Economic Growth." *Journal of Economic History* 65 (2005): 285–351.

North, Douglass C. *Institutions, Institutional Change, and Economic Performance.* Cambridge: Cambridge University Press. 1999.

———. *Understanding the Process of Economic Change.* Princeton: Princeton University Press, 2005.

Olson, Mancur. *The Logic of Collective Action: Public Goods and the Theory of Groups.* 2d ed. New York: Schocken Books, 1971.

Rivoli, Pietra. *The Travels of a T-Shirt in the Global Economy: An Economist Examines the Markets, Power, and Politics of World Trade.* Hoboken: John Wiley & Sons, 2005.

Schumpeter, Joseph A. *Capitalism, Socialism and Democracy.* 3d ed. New York: Harper & Row, 1950.

Schweikart, Larry. *The Entrepreneurial Adventure: A History of Business in the United States.* Orlando: Harcourt Brace, 2000.

Seabright, Paul. *The Company of Strangers: A Natural History of Economic Life.* Princeton: Princeton University Press, 2004.

Smith, Adam. *An Inquiry into the Nature and Causes of the Wealth of Nations.* Chicago: University of Chicago Press, 1976.

Index

About the Author

BRADLEY A. HANSEN is Associate Professor and Chair, Department of Economics, University of Mary Washington, where he has taught since 1995. He previously served on the faculty of Moorhead State University and as a senior teaching fellow at Washington University. He is the author of many articles, book chapters, research papers, and conference presentations on economic policy and social welfare.